The Year of the Trout

The Year of the Trout

Steve Raymond

with illustrations
by Dave Whitlock

WINCHESTER PRESS
An Imprint of New Century Publishers, Inc.

For my mother
GRACE A. RAYMOND

Printing Code
11 12 13 14 15 16

Library of Congress Cataloging in Publication Data
Raymond, Steve.
   The year of the trout.

   1. Trout fishing. I. Title.
SH687.R39   1985   799.1'755   85-6155
ISBN 0-8329-0384-1

Contents

Summer

Fall

Credits

Some portions of this book were published previously in various magazines or periodicals or are based on works by the author published in such form.

"The Next Best Thing" is based partly on "An Angling Library for the '80s," originally published in *The Flyfisher*, Vol. XVI, No. 4, 1983.

"Cutthroat Slough" originally appeared in slightly condensed form in *Fly Fisherman Magazine*, Vol. 14, No. 3, May 1983.

"Like Father, Like Son" first appeared as "The Legacy" in the July 1982 issue of *PSA Magazine*, carried aboard Pacific Southwest Airline.

"Fishing the Misty Fjords" originally was published in slightly different form in *The Flyfisher*, Vol. XII, No. 3, 1979.

The account of the eruption of Mount St. Helens in "Pages from a Trout Fisherman's Diary" is adapted from "A Day of Fishing Became A Night of Fear," first published in *Sports Illustrated,* July 14, 1980.

"The Once and Future River" is adapted from "It Was A Sad Day for A Fisherman When the Green River Lost Its Glitter," first published in *Sports Illustrated,* October 20, 1980.

"Hello Dolly!" is expanded from an article first published as "Hello, Dolly, It's So Nice to Have You Back," in *Sports Illustrated,* March 26, 1979.

"Blackberry Run" was first published in *Fly Fisherman Magazine,* Vol. 14, No. 5, July 1983.

Portions of "Fall Favorite" are adapted from "The Dry Fly in Salt Water," first published in *Fly Fisherman Magazine*, Vol. 10, No. 3, March 1979.

"A Fish to Remember" was first published in slightly different form as "A Steelheader's Autumn" in *Fly Fisherman Magazine*, Vol. 11, No. 1, October-December 1979.

Acknowledgments

Many persons made generous contributions of time and information to this book. I am especially indebted to Professor Charles J. (Jack) Smiley of the University of Idaho for sharing his findings from the fossil site at Miocene Clarkia Lake and for showing me the site and the surrounding countryside. A special word of thanks also is due Professor Smiley and his family for their warm and generous hospitality.

I am deeply grateful to Dr. Robert J. Behnke of the Department of Fishery and Wildlife Biology at Colorado State University for his advice and for permission to quote from his published research. His monograph on Western trouts was of invaluable assistance in preparing the chapter on the evolutionary history of trout, and his careful study of the history of the Lahontan cutthroat trout provided much of the information reported in the chapter on that fish. Without Dr. Behnke's generous help, it's safe to say this book would have been two chapters shorter.

Dr. Gerald R. Smith of the University of Michigan Museum of Paleontology also was most helpful in answering my questions about the evolutionary relationships of trout and provided a great deal of valuable information on recent fossil trout discoveries. It also was Dr. Smith who examined and identified the fossil fish from Miocene Clarkia Lake and suggested its possible history.

A word of extra thanks is due to all three men for reading, criticizing and suggesting changes to the chapters on the Clarkia fish and the trout family tree. They share no accountability for any conclusions or opinions expressed in those chapters, however; I am solely responsible for those.

Others who provided generous assistance were Bill Rember of the University of Idaho and Dr. Fred Utter of the National Marine Fisheries Service in Seattle, plus the efficient staffs of the Libraries of Fisheries and Natural Sciences at the University of Washington.

I shall always be grateful to Dale Pihlman and Tom Ramiskey for arranging the trip that led to the chapter on "Fishing the Misty Fjords." I wish only that I could have found more vivid words to describe that wonderful country.

James G. Swan's account of the Chehalis River treaty council, quoted in "Steelhead Blues," is a brief excerpt from his long and colorful diary of life on the Northwest frontier. Swan's diary, now in the public domain, has been published in book form by the University of Washington Press under the title of *The Northwest Coast, or Three Years' Residence in Washington Territory*. Anyone with an interest in the history of the region will find it worth reading.

Finally, to my wife, Joan, and my children, Stephanie and Randy, some very special words of thanks for being so patient and understanding.

Steve Raymond

Preface

A new book by Steve Raymond is always an angling-literary event. For Steve is that rare blend of angler *and* writer, a man who knows and loves his fishing intimately and who writes of it with deft skill. And since he writes too little, any new book—and especially one this fine—is all the more to be cherished.

In *The Year of the Trout* he follows the seasons, as he did in *The Year of the Angler*, but here the focus is more persistently outside, less on the man than on his quarry and on the world of his pursuit. Steelhead, brook trout, Dolly Varden, Atlantic salmon transplanted to a western lake, rainbows, cutthroats, and browns—we find these, in their seasons (especially the steelhead, which Steve chiefly loves), and we find also the special places in which they live. Like all of us who fish, Steve has a deep affection for those "lonely, wild, and beautiful" places, and through the year he finds us a full measure of these in which to fish.

Steve Raymond is a writer on whom little in the natural world, or in the experience of fishing, is lost: the cryptic codes on the surface of a river, the history of a particular fallen tree on which he's chanced to sit, the dramatic early life of the steelhead he's tenaciously pursued and finally caught. He is always interested in the "now"—in what's before him—but also, always, in what has gone before and what someday will be. So you get a special density in a Steve Raymond book, quite unlike that in any other angling writing I know—a movement into the natural world in which its author stands, a movement back into the history of a place or thing, and, always, a solicitude for the future.

Often, as in his writing on New Zealand and the Misty Fjords area of Alaska, you feel a past that will never truly be past pushing up against a present that is more than it seems merely to the senses. So the angler's New Zealand that everyone writes about these days is only a part of what Steve offers; we also get a textured history of several hundred years, only some of which is even associated with trout. And we hear, in other instances, of lesser known little rivers and their historical origins, of matters paleontological, and, of course—because he has long been one of our finest book reviewers—of books, which are crucially part of the history, the substance, the world of angling, and where the past also presses up into the current moment.

But the most vivid parts of this wonderful book, like those parts in any fine book about fly fishing, are the worlds of the angler and his quarry, in the present. We get winter steelhead on a day so cold the author's fingers, as he tied on a new leader and fly, were so numb he lit a pipe for warmth; then he cupped his "frozen hands around its bowl to feel the heat come slowly through the brier." We get winter cutthroat in an Indian slough, too—and some unexpected new friends. We get that special bond between father and son, built uniquely by fishing. "Call it an attitude or feeling," Steve writes, "a sort of inner excitement that returns each spring when the green buds burst open on the trees, the mayflies hatch, and trout begin to rise. It's that and more—a kind of understanding and appreciation that fishing is one of the very best things that ever a man can do, and trout fishing is the very best of all. It is one of my father's most precious gifts to me, and now I hope somehow to impart the same feelings to my son."

That's fine, memorable prose, isn't it?

But we also get a special "birthday trout," a gift to make us smile, and we get an inutterably sad and moving description of a trout river devastated by the eruption of Mt. St. Helens. "It was a dead river," Steve says, "flowing through a dead land."

One of my favorite sections treats his diaries—with pages in one that still have trout scales stuck to them, and a motto that such a book, an angling diary, is not to be measured "by how much information it can hold, but how well it preserves the memories of a fishing lifetime." And I am especially moved by the section on his fishing camp, bought from friends with whom he has shared wonderful days astream, blessed finally by a visit with the ashes of one of those old, dear friends.

What a wonderful trip, then, this book offers. We travel from the icy days of one winter until the final changes of another fall are registered in the chill air and the colors of the cottonwoods. Along the way we see lots of new water, feel the powerful fight of a sea-fresh steelhead, slip back into the past, laugh and cry a little, and catch some memorable fish.

How I'd like to have spent that year fishing for these trout with Steve!

But maybe, through this splendid book, I have. And so will you.

NICK LYONS

Winter

T he days of winter seem so short yet the season seems so long. The mornings are calm and cold, with frost forming beneath a floating layer of mist. The woods are still, the streams dark and low with a grudging flow of water from the snowfields on the foothill slopes. But the trout are there.

Perhaps nothing is as deceiving as the appearance of a winter stream. Though the trees along its banks are barren, though the snow reaches down to the water's edge, though the river itself seems slow and dark and sullen, beneath the surface there is abundant life. True, there is less of it and it moves at a slower pace than in summer rivers; yet still it moves. Though the earth seems to hold its breath in winter, the cycle of predator and prey, of life and death and procreation still goes on in the rivers. And the trout are always there.

The steelhead returns in winter. It has done so since long before calendars were kept, for with its instincts it has no need to number days. But now men know the timing of its ways and wait with rod and reel and feathered fly to greet the first returning fish, still sea-fresh and shining bright.

They also know the ways of all the other kinds of trout and seek each one in its proper season. They know the landlocked rainbow usually is a bold and reckless fish, at its best in the spring when the mayflies and sedges are hatching; and yet they know too that sometimes the rainbow may be as elusive as its name, a momentary bend of color in the sky, then vanished.

They know the cutthroat as a clan of many cousins, each a little different from all the rest, yet each a practical, pragmatic fish that makes the most of things in almost any season, in saltwater or in fresh. They know the brown trout as a street-wise fish, cunning, tough, and smart. A wary brown is a challenge for any fisherman and 'rare is the angler who does not respect it.

They know the golden trout is as spectacular as its name suggests and as rare as a gleaming nugget in the gravel of a mountain stream—and just as much worth finding. They know the Atlantic salmon is a grand fish that does things on a grand scale, that it is the largest of all the trouts and a great prize for any angler. They know the brook trout really is a char, but one that has earned a trout's name, a fish of unsurpassed beauty and grace.

All these they know as members of the bright firmament of fish called trout. And from the very first cold dawn of winter to the very last gray twilight of the fall, men seek them through the changing seasons of The Year of the Trout.

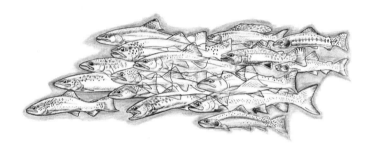

Upstream Journey

Snow had fallen overnight, a soft wet snow that pressed heavily on fir and cedar limbs and broke off and fell in cold little clots as I passed through the woods on the way to the river. The highway was a long way off, the river was quiet within its channel somewhere up ahead and there was not a sound to disturb the tranquility of the cold, empty morning.

A pair of anglers had preceded me along the snowy trail, leaving a double set of footprints, but where the trail forked near the river I was relieved to see that both had turned downstream. I was headed for an upstream drift, hoping for a steelhead to start the year.

I found the familiar path bordering the river and picked my way over slippery, snow-covered rocks and fallen logs, grasping the trunk of a friendly alder and using it as a lever to swing across a place where some past flood had washed away the trail. Other anglers who had passed this way had done the same for so many seasons that their hands had worn a groove in the alder's trunk.

I walked a mile or more before I came upon the run. It looked as I remembered it from times before, 200 yards of good steelhead water, shallow on my side but dropping steeply to a deep slot against the far bank. But one thing was new: Halfway down the run a tree had dug itself top-first into the river bottom and now its drowned trunk angled up through the water and its roots tilted crazily out of the current. It would be a difficult place to fish without hanging up a fly, but the tree would offer shelter where a steelhead might hold; it would be a place worth fishing.

I walked up to the head of the drift and waded in slowly, gauging the strength of the current and feeling its chill come quickly through my waders. Then I stripped out the fast-sinking line and began casting a big bright fly, quartering downstream and lengthening line until the fly was dropping within a foot or two of the high bank on the far side. The current was swift and acted quickly on the line. Each cast required two or three quick upstream mends to hold the fly where I wanted it, to give it a chance to sink to the depth where a steelhead might be waiting.

But if any were waiting, they ignored the fly as I fished through the upper part of the run. Near the middle of the drift the current quickened even more, so I switched to upstream casts to give the fly more time to sink. After the first two or three of these the line drew slowly tight against a weight that wouldn't yield; somewhere, down below, the fly had found a snag. I worked hard to free it, but in the end there was nothing left to do but break it off and go ashore to replace the leader tippet and the fly.

As I waded out I noticed a large log lying near the water's edge. It was just the right size for sitting, so I sat down and fumbled in the bulging pockets of my fishing vest for a spool of the right-sized leader material. I found it and cut off a measured length, but my fingers were so nearly numb it took three tries to tie the knot to join it to the remnant of leader the river had left me. It was a similar chore to tie on a duplicate of the fly I'd lost, so after that I reached again inside my vest and found the old tobacco pouch and battered pipe. I filled the pipe and lit it, then cupped my frozen hands around its bowl to feel the heat come slowly through the brier.

I watched the river as I waited for my hands to warm; its surface spelled out hurried messages in a cryptic code, erased them, then quickly wrote others in their place. Beyond the stream, a line of cottonwoods stretched naked limbs against a leaden sky and the ground still was bleak and white with snow.

I chanced to look down at the log upon which I sat. It was a stout log, splintered at each end, but the river's abrasive silt had long ago worn away the splintered ends to harmless rounded stubs. Still, it was obvious this was a broken section of what once had been a large and substantial tree.

I brushed away some snow to see if I could tell what sort of tree it might have been, but the wood beneath was old and gray, weathered and bleached by countless days of sun and wind and current. It had been tossed against a hundred gravel bars and beaches, and particles of sand and silt had worn its surface smooth—so smooth it was hard to see the grain of wood, hard to tell what kind of wood it was. But whatever sort of tree it once had been, the splintered ends were proof that it had not been cut by saw or ax; some natural force had brought it down.

I wondered what that force was and when and where it had happened. For how many scores of years had the tree lived? Had it stood proudly near the river, watching salmon and steelhead passing upstream and their offspring coming down, season after season, until suddenly a great spring flood had reached out and claimed it? Had it once grown straight and tall on a windward hillside, stretching its limbs among eagles? Had lightning brought it down, or fire, or a great wind? Or had it merely died a quiet, natural death and gone on standing until weather, birds and insects turned it to a gaunt old snag, a tombstone to itself, before it finally fell?

All questions without answers. And yet for some reason I wanted to know the answers, wanted to know where this tree had lived and how it had died and what convoluted route it had followed to this place.

Perhaps the strange handwriting of the river held the answers, but if so I could not read them.

The last tobacco had burned out of my pipe and the river beckoned, so I stood, stiff from cold, moved around a bit to loosen up, then waded once more into the current and resumed casting. At first nothing happened, and after a while my mind began to wander as I settled into the mechanical routine of casting so that I failed to notice when the line came to a slow and subtle stop at the end of a long cast. The line began to move upstream, slowly at first, then with increasing speed, and in the instant I took to ponder this development the line came tight and suddenly the reel was spinning wildly.

I raised the rod then and felt furious resistance. The line already was off the reel and the backing followed swiftly as I started for the beach. Then the long run finally ended and the fish broached in the current, far upstream, and I caught a glimpse of its silver shape.

A hooked steelhead that runs upstream places itself at a disadvantage, for it must contend with both angler and current. This one quickly realized its error and changed directions, heading downstream so rapidly that a dangerous belly formed in the trailing line. I cranked the reel as quickly as I could until finally the line came tight again, though it slanted downstream at a dangerous angle.

I followed the fish down, putting on all the strain I dared to keep it from the hazard of the drowned tree in the center of the run. The fish came reluctantly away from the snag, then turned and ran once more, and again I was forced to follow. It was a stubborn fish, strong and determined to keep its freedom, but the unyielding spring of the long rod finally proved stronger; the steelhead turned on its side and I led it carefully into quiet water and eased it up onto the snow-covered river rocks along the beach.

It was a classic sea-fresh winter fish, slim and bright steel-gray on its back and gleaming nickel on its sides. I judged it was easily eight pounds. Carefully I twisted the fly free from its jaw, then held the fish gently in the shallow water. The decision to release it had long ago been made, but I found myself holding it for a long time, admiring its beauty and graceful shape as I eased it back and forth to restore rhythm to the movement of its gills. Slowly its movements grew stronger and at last I let it go; it swam slowly outward and down along the sloping cobble bottom.

I watched it go and thought of the path it had followed to reach this place. Like the log behind me on the beach, the stream had borne it down from the hills, yet unlike the log the fish had come willingly and with purpose. It had reached the sea and gone about its life's clear and uncomplicated mission: to forage in the rich ocean pastures, to survive and grow, and finally to return to its native river and spawn. I had briefly interrupted its progress toward this goal, but now it was free to resume its upstream journey and complete its purpose. And if it did, it could then die peacefully with whatever dim sense of accomplishment a trout may have.

I thought of my own life in comparison with the steelhead's and of the course that had brought me to this cold and quiet beach on a winter morning. It was a course infinitely more complicated than the trout's, filled with unexpected twists and sudden turns, false starts and fitful purposes, satisfying advances and sorry retreats. It also was a course without a clear and certain purpose, for unlike the steelhead a man has no familiar river to which one day he knows he will return. A steelhead always knows where it is going, but a man seldom does.

I rested for a while and smoked another pipe, then waded in and fished out the remainder of the run, but no more fish touched my fly. The morning was well spent, the overcast showed signs of breaking and the snow had begun melting from the sagging limbs along the river. The stream continued to scrawl its mysterious moving messages, but their meaning was no clearer now than it had been before. I decided it was time to move on, to head upstream and try another pool and see what surprises it might hold in store.

I walked up from the tail of the long run, past the submerged tree with its roots waving in the current, past the spot where I had hooked the fish, on up to the point where the trail disappeared among the trees. For some reason I paused there and took a last look back and my eye fell upon the log still resting on the beach.

The snow had melted from it and it looked different with its dull bleached wood gleaming darkly through the wet. It lay there, an unknown soldier of the woods, waiting for the river to bear it to some final resting place far from its home. I wondered how long its wait would be, and how many more seasons it would spend on lonely beaches before it finally reached the end of its halting, uncertain journey.

Then I turned away and continued upstream on an uncertain journey of my own. But I was pleased; I had taken the first fish of a new year, a good and satisfying fish, and upstream, through the woods, I could see the sky was bright.

The Land of the Long White Cloud

Back home the winter winds were blowing and the rivers were in flood, but it was early summer in New Zealand and the morning air was fresh and sweet as I stepped for the first time into the Major Jones Pool of the Tongariro River. After only a few casts I hooked a strong fish that fought with all the vigor of a fresh-run steelhead, as indeed its ancestors once had been.

In all, five bright rainbows took my fly on that first pass through the Major Jones, one of the most famous trout pools on earth, and I marveled at the fact that it was possible for an angler to trade seasons and travel to the Southern Hemisphere to find trout fishing such as this.

New Zealand now is justly famous as a Mecca for trout fishermen, though its rich waters have held trout only a little more than a hundred years and the country itself was not discovered by European explorers until the 17th century. But its history reaches back much further and it is a history worth knowing—a fascinating story that begins in misty legends a thousand years old, passed down from generation to generation in tales told over campfires in the long antipodean twilights.

By most accounts, it began with a voyage from a legendary island known as Hawaiki, somewhere in eastern Polynesia. There, it is said, a warrior named Kupe murdered a carver named Hoturapa, took Hotura-pa's wife and escaped in the slain man's canoe. Learning of this, Hotura-pa's relatives gave pursuit, chasing the fugitive pair far across the ocean until they finally were lost from sight.

For day after day and week after week, Kupe and his consort traveled across the long rolling swells of the South Pacific with only flying fish and porpoises for company. Each morning the sun rose at their backs and each evening it beckoned them onward as it sank, blood-red, back into the restless sea. Ever southwestward they sailed, across the lonely heaving landscape of the ocean, until at last came a morning when the far horizon was hidden by a long layer of white cloud—perhaps a sign of land!

With gathering hope and excitement, Kupe and his woman sailed on until they were close enough to see there *was* land ahead—a great land that stretched beyond sight both to the north and south, a land of high forested hills that rose to the dim and distant shapes of enormous mountains far inland. And when Hoturapa's canoe finally grated safely on the sand and Kupe stepped ashore, he was ready with a name for the new-found land: Aotearoa, the Land of the Long White Cloud.

Kupe's tale is apocryphal, one of many legends about the settlement of Aotearoa. Another version suggests that Kupe returned to Hawaiki and told others about Aotearoa so they were later able to find it for themselves. The exact truth probably never will be known, but there is little doubt that sometime within the past 600 to 1,000 years at least one canoe, and perhaps many, traveled from somewhere in east Polynesia to the myste-rious country far to the southwest.

The newcomers found a magnificent land of two great islands and many smaller ones, covered with thick forests and stands of giant ferns and riven by cold, rushing rivers that hurried down from the hills. One of the big islands had a volcanic spine, a chain of fiery mountains, geysers, steaming lakes, and strange pools of boiling mud, and right in the middle of it was a great blue inland sea. The other island had a range of even higher mountains, glacier-crested peaks that disappeared into perpetual cloud, and a ragged coastline punctured by deep saltwater fjords with lush rain forests growing down to their shores. In the forests lived parrots, parakeets, and a whole galaxy of other birds.

But the new arrivals also found they were not the first people to reach this land. Some earlier migration, now forgotten even in legend, had brought primitive tribes that lived by hunting enormous emu-like flightless birds called moas, some standing as much as ten feet tall—the largest birds ever to live on earth. The primitive culture of these tribes was no match for the more advanced Polynesian way of life, and as the newcomers spread out to occupy the islands, the moa hunters slowly melted away until both they and the moas were extinct.

The Polynesians brought with them food-bearing plants and a tradition of agriculture, but they also were skilled fishermen and found bountiful harvests of fish in the seas around the new land. They also found rich, oily eels that migrated into the rivers; a small fish they called Inanga that entered the estuaries in great numbers every spring, and a handsome, grayling-like fish called the Upokororo that followed the Inanga and fed upon its schools. They also learned to spear or snare the abundant waterfowl and birds, and occasionally they augmented their largely meatless diet by eating one another. They called themselves the Maori.

For several hundred years the Maori had Aotearoa to themselves. But in 1642 the Dutch East India Company sent out two ships under command of Abel Tasman to search for new lands in the South Pacific, and on December 13 of that year Tasman sighted the west coast of the southern great island of Aotearoa, which he recorded as "a large land uplifted high." His first contact with the Maoris ended in a violent clash in which four of Tasman's men were killed, and the explorer sailed away without ever setting foot on his discovery.

Over the next 150 years Aotearoa was visited by other explorers flying British, French, and Spanish flags. By 1790 New Zealand—as it was then called in Europe—was considered fair game for exploitation by the outside world. Hundreds of vessels arrived to begin hunting the fur seals that clustered on the South Island beaches and these were quickly followed by whaling ships and timber traders.

Close on the heels of the exploiters came Anglican, Wesleyan, and Catholic missionaries bent on bringing God's word to the Maoris. They sent back tales of tragedy and atrocity, and these stories, combined with concerns over French territorial ambitions in the South Pacific, prompted a reluctant British government to annex New Zealand. Capt. William

Hobson of the Royal Navy was sent to negotiate a treaty with the Maori chiefs for transfer of sovereignty to Britain; the result was the 1840 Treaty of Waitangi, which opened the way for full British settlement of New Zealand.

In the years following, as more and more British colonists arrived, they began yearning for two of the favorite things the British already had carried to so many other far-flung lands: tea and trout.

New Zealand's climate and waters seemed ideally suited for trout. In fact, the colonists found one trout-like fish already living there, the fish the Maoris had called the Upokororo and which the settlers soon named the New Zealand grayling. Formally classified *Prototroctes oxyrhynchus*, it was a curious fish, growing as large as 18 inches and appearing in lowland streams during the summer and fall, then disappearing during the winter only to turn up again in the spring to feed on schools of young Inanga in the estuaries. The Inanga itself, *Galaxiias attenuatus*, was called "whitebait" by the settlers. It was one of a number of galaxiids—slim, scaleless pike-like fish—common to New Zealand's streams and lakes.

But the New Zealand grayling had little opportunity to prove any sporting qualities it may have had. Along with the whitebait it was considered an excellent food fish, and both species were netted in great numbers when the whitebait were running. Catches were so plentiful that surplus fish sometimes were used as fertilizer in colonists' gardens. This kind of heavy pressure, combined with changes to the environment and other factors, was too much for the New Zealand grayling; its numbers dwindled rapidly and it soon became rare.

But even if the New Zealand grayling had fared better it almost certainly would not have made the colonists forget their favorite fish. The task of obtaining trout from overseas sources was taken on by local "acclimatisation societies," groups of sportsmen organized expressly for the purpose of bringing in exotic species of game and fish to improve sporting opportunities in New Zealand.

In 1867, the Canterbury Acclimatisation Society obtained brown trout eggs from Tasmania, where trout had been introduced three years earlier. The eggs were hatched at the society's pond in Hagley Park in Christchurch on the South Island, but only three fish survived and all three managed to escape into a nearby swamp. Two were later recaptured, and by great good fortune one was male and the other female. They were returned to the hatchery, presumably under better security, and over the next few years they provided many offspring for stocking in Canterbury waters.

In 1870, the Auckland Acclimatisation Society introduced brown trout to the North Island. These fish also were hatched from eggs received from Tasmania, the source of all the brown trout stocked in New Zealand until 1883. In that year the Dunedin and Wellington Acclimatisation Societies imported a shipment of eggs directly from Loch Leven in Scotland. Later shipments came from Rhine River stock and from Italian waters.

But brown trout alone were not enough to satisfy the members of the acclimatisation societies. They were eager to import other species as well.

The Auckland society's minute book for August 1878 records the arrival of a shipment of eggs from Lake Tahoe, California, a gift from a Mr. T. Russell. After hatching, 2,000 fry survived and it was left to the society's chairman to decide where they should be released; unfortunately the minute book contains no record of his decision.

There also remains some question about just what kind of trout these were. At the time, and for many years afterward, it was generally assumed they were rainbows, but that assumption has been challenged by recent research. In findings published in 1978, D. Scott, J. Hewitson and J.C. Fraser pointed out that it now appears doubtful rainbow trout ever were indigenous to Lake Tahoe, but the Lahontan cutthroat, *Salmo clarki henshawi*, was native; therefore, the trout imported by the Auckland society may very well have been Lahontan cutthroat. If indeed that was the case, there is no record of what finally became of these fish; presumably they either died out or were absorbed through hybridization into rainbow trout populations introduced later.

For its next shipment the Auckland Society decided that it wanted Eastern brook trout (char) from the United States. The minute book for April 3, 1883, reports "the Secretary announced the arrival of 10,000 brook trout ova from San Francisco by the *City of New York*, from which 500 healthy young fish had been hatched, and also of 12,000 ova of the same fish by the *Zealandia*, about 5,000 or 6,000 of which appeared in good condition."

At first these fish did well in the Auckland Society's ponds, but the following spring brought unusually warm weather and soon dead trout fingerlings were found floating in the ponds. Society members quickly transferred the survivors to cooler ponds along the Waihou River near Okoroire, 120 miles south. There they survived and flourished and many subsequently were released into North Island rivers.

Some fish were kept for breeding stock, however, and by 1886, when they were starting to reach sexual maturity, their appearance was beginning to puzzle members of the society. The minute book for September 7, 1886, describes them as "black-spotted Brook trout," although the true Eastern brook trout has no black spots. Later it became clear these fish were actually rainbow trout and the 1883 shipments represented the first successful introduction of rainbows in New Zealand.

For many years it was accepted as gospel that the eggs in these shipments had come from steelhead in California's Russian River. But the research of Scott, Hewitson, and Fraser turned up convincing evidence that they actually came from a run of winter steelhead returning to Sonoma Creek, a tributary of San Francisco Bay. Confirmation is found in a report published in the *Sonoma County Weekly Index* on July 21, 1883:

"Mr. A.V. La Motte, superintendent of the Lenni Fish Propagating Company, informs us that the company sometime since shipped 30,000 trout eggs to the Auckland, New Zealand, Acclimatisation Society, and have received the report from them that they arrived in better order than any prior lot they had received from other parties. This we consider another feather in Sonoma's cap, and a big, bright one, too." La Motte's hatchery was on Sonoma Creek, although much later he operated a hatchery on the Russian River—a fact which probably explains the long confusion over the source of New Zealand's first rainbows.

But no matter where they came from, brown and rainbow trout adapted quickly to New Zealand's cold, fertile rivers and lakes, finding abundant food in the native smelt, galaxiid, crayfish, and insect populations. Some grew to phenomenal size in a remarkably short time; in 1891 anglers reported catching rainbows weighing up to 9 pounds in Lake Takapuna on the North Island, and in 1892 a 28-pound brown trout was taken from Butel's Creek, a tributary of Lake Hayes near Queenstown on the South Island.

Perhaps the most spectacular fishing developed in and around Lake Taupo, the great blue 400-square-mile inland sea of the North Island. Taupo is fed by scores of rivers and streams, most notably the charming little Waitahanui, the gentle Hatepe, the tranquil Tauranga Taupo, and the big, swift Tongariro. The first brown trout were released in Lake Taupo by the Auckland Acclimatisation Society in 1886, and 11 years later the Wellington Society liberated rainbow trout in the lake. The rainbow, descended from the original 1883 Sonoma Creek shipments, quickly reverted to the migratory habits of their ancestral stock, feeding on the rich store of natural food in the lake, then migrating up its tributary streams to spawn.

O.S. "Budge" Hintz, New Zealand's best-known angling author, relates an early record of the fishing at Taupo from the diary of a British angler named King-Webster. On his first visit in 1908 King-Webster traveled 56 miles by horse-drawn coach from Rotorua to the town of Taupo on the northeastern shore of the lake, then by steamer the length of the lake to the settlement of Tokaanu near the mouth of the Tongariro at the lake's south end. "King-Webster fished triumphantly, at times almost incredulously, on the Tongariro," Hintz wrote. "Fish running into double-figure weight were common, and his best was one of 19 pounds."

King-Webster also spent three days fishing the Waitahanui, which drains the volcanic slopes on the eastern shore of Lake Taupo. During those three days he took 17 fish with a combined weight of 166 pounds. His best was a 14-pound rainbow taken from the little Mangamutu Stream which enters the Waitahanui just before the latter flows into the lake.

Another early visitor to the Waitahanui was Major Percy Stewart, who recorded his adventures in a 1924 book, *Round the World with Rod and Rifle*. Stewart made four trips to the Waitahanui during the years 1909-1914. On his first visit he caught trout averaging slightly more than 10 pounds, but on subsequent trips he noted a gradual decline in the size of the trout until by 1914 the average weight was only five pounds.

There is a famous, oft-published photograph taken in 1911 of a pair of Taupo anglers displaying a single day's catch of 78 trout taken at the mouth of Waihaha Stream, another Taupo tributary. Seventeen of these fish weighed 16 pounds or more; none was less than 12 pounds.

But the native Maoris who lived around the lake accounted for the largest catches. There are stories of a 37½-pound rainbow taken by Maoris from Mangamutu Stream and of a huge, 51½-pound brown trout captured near the south end of Lake Taupo. Like Kupe's tale, however, these stories are largely apocryphal.

Whatever the truth, by all accounts the early-century fishing in Lake Taupo was nothing short of incredible. But as Major Stewart's records indicate, a rapid decline in the average size of trout was becoming evident as early as 1914. Soon it became apparent the trout had succeeded only too well in taking advantage of the hundreds of miles of spawning water in Taupo's tributaries and had reproduced at an explosive rate. Their rapidly increasing numbers had seriously depleted the lake's great store of natural food, something no one had ever thought possible. By 1918 the average weight of Taupo trout had fallen to a little over three pounds.

Commercial netting for trout was allowed in the lake starting in

1913, but at first there was little market for the fish and few were taken. But as more shipments made their way to the cities, demand increased and the numbers of trout taken went up rapidly. By 1921, when commercial fishing was halted, the trout population had been thinned to the point that equilibrium with the food supply had been restored; the average weight of Taupo trout in that year was between five and seven pounds and by 1924 it topped 10 pounds. In 1926, three anglers took 450 pounds of trout from the Tongariro in a single day.

But it took only a decade for the trout population to build itself back to the point where the balance of the lake again was disturbed. By 1939 the average weight of Taupo trout had declined to about four pounds, and in an effort to reverse the trend the government began transplanting native smelt from the Rotorua lakes into Lake Taupo. Gradually the smelt took hold in their new home and began to multiply and the trout turned to them as a new source of food. The average weight of trout slowly increased until it leveled off at around five pounds. It has remained close to that figure ever since.

The advent of jet travel in recent years has made New Zealand a favorite refuge for anglers seeking escape from the Northern Hemisphere winter. The South Island fishery, still primarily for brown trout, usually is best in January and February, when the northern winter is at its worst. The best fishing on the North Island comes a bit later when the Lake Taupo rainbows begin running to the tributaries, and the runs peak in the early southern winter months of May and June. Lately, however, Taupo fishermen have noted increasing numbers of bright fish entering the Tongariro as late as spring or even early summer.

It was one of these late runs of rainbow that greeted me that first memorable morning on the Major Jones Pool. The smallest fish was a little over three pounds, the largest a little over five, and all behaved with the explosive violence I have learned to expect from sea-run rainbows in the brawling rivers of the Pacific Northwest.

I landed the last fish just above the tail-out of the pool, then found a place to rest in the shade and watch other anglers work their way through the long curving reach of the Major Jones. They were the latest in a long line of Taupo anglers dating back to the days of Major Stewart, King-Webster and before, and I was glad to be among them—glad to find my own small place in the century-old tradition of fishing for transplanted trout in the Land of the Long White Cloud.

The Next Best Thing

A good fishing book is a joy in itself, but a good book is even better when it is read in front of a warm fire on a long winter evening while the wind is strong and rain is rattling like buckshot on the windowpanes. A book read under such circumstances can very easily become a magic thing, lifting the reader's mind and carrying him forward to the pleasures that await on spring ponds and summer rivers, or transporting him back to memories of past rewarding days. Books speak to us of all the mysteries that make trout fishing such a captivating sport; next to fishing itself, there is nothing better than a good fishing book.

There are many to choose from. In terms of importance, fishing can scarcely be said to rank with such matters as war or statecraft, but the literature of angling is hardly less extensive than the literature for either of those subjects. Fishing for trout has prompted as much study and debate as any of the arts or sciences; it has evolved its own philosophy and ethics, its own customs and codes, its own language and technology, and all of these are described in books.

It's often said that a trout fisherman passes through a predictable evolution, starting with a desire to catch as many fish as possible and working up to a point where he ignores all but the most difficult or demanding fish. I believe a student of angling literature must pass through a similar metamorphosis. It begins with an indiscriminate desire to read as many fishing books as possible, then progresses through stages of increasing selectivity until it finally culminates in a preference for the most challenging or thoughtful works. At least that has been true in my case.

The first fishing book I ever read was Zane Grey's *Tales of Fresh-Water Fishing*. I was no more than 10 years old when I found the tall green volume in my father's library and took it down from the shelf. Grey's prose style was flamboyant, sometimes given to exaggeration or extreme, but I didn't realize it then; to me his book was a collection of thrilling angling tales in which I could easily imagine myself as the central character. Thanks to my father's interest in fishing I already had gained a fair amount of experience with trout, but Grey's book provided an inkling that there was more to the business of fishing than I had supposed.

The next angling book I read was Roderick Haig-Brown's classic *A River Never Sleeps*, which broadened my horizons much further. Haig-Brown articulated many things about fishing that I was beginning to sense or feel but had yet to translate into thoughts or concepts of my own. His book was full of rich feeling and warm expression; it was an ideal book for an angler to read in his formative years, and though I have since reread it many times, I always have been glad that I first came upon it when I did.

After my early acquaintance with Grey and Haig-Brown, I began haunting the aisles of the public library, checking out all the fishing books I could find on the shelves. It was a mixed bag if ever there was one; I found myself reading not only about trout, but also about salmon, tarpon, bonefish, bass and other species. Some of the books were just awful— there is no other honest way to describe them—and some were about fish or fishing I would never likely see or do. But they were all about fishing, and so I read all of them faithfully.

It did not take very long to read most of the fishing books the library had to offer (there were others listed in the card catalogue that I wanted very much to read, but the fishermen who borrowed them never brought them back. That suggested a lesson: Never loan a book to a fisherman). And the more I read, the more I began to understand which authors and which books had most to offer, or which ones were held in highest regard by other writers. With this knowledge I was able to begin reading more selectively, and since the only way I could obtain some of the books I wanted was to buy them, I finally took the ultimate step and started an angling library of my own.

It was a small thing at first, just a few volumes tucked between a flimsy pair of bookends on a single shelf, but over the years it has grown massively until it now occupies a full wall of shelves in my office. During the time it took to reach such size its contents changed character many times, always reflecting my current interests—and that, I think, is what a good library should do.

But every library also should contain at least a few of the truly seminal works on angling. By these I mean books that were first to express important new ideas—Halford's works on the dry fly, Skues on the nymph, Jock Scott on the greased-line method, La Branche on the dry fly in American waters, Jennings and his successors on trout-fly entomology, Marinaro on minutae—to mention just a few.

Studying the works of these masters also is likely to stimulate a reader's interest in history and the cultivation of such an interest is the next logical step in becoming a literate angler. The scholarly works of John Waller Hills, John McDonald, William Radcliffe, and Alfred Joshua Butler together will provide an angler with a solid background in the origins and development of the sport. Arnold Gingrich's *The Fishing in Print* also qualifies here because Gingrich, in summarizing the work of nearly every important fishing writer, managed to span most of the known history of angling—and angling literature and history often are synonymous.

Many fishing books are of the instructional variety, and any student of the sport should begin by reading some of these. It is not necessary to read very many in order to become thoroughly grounded in the principles and techniques of trout fishing, and one would not really wish to read too many or he would soon begin to notice a depressing similarity among them. Most cover essentially the same ground, often in the same way, sometimes even in the same words. Such books are necessary, but they do not represent angling literature at its best. I keep some in my library, not because I enjoy reading them but because they are valuable for reference; if I need to know how to dress a certain fly or tie a certain knot, I know that somewhere in these books I will find the answer.

The highest level of expression in angling literature is found in books about the philosophy and appreciation of the sport. These subjects have inspired more eloquence than any others, and in dealing with them some writers have found ways to touch a reader's heart and soul.

A River Never Sleeps would have to rank near the top of any list of such books. It is generally considered Haig-Brown's greatest work, but he produced many other classics of nearly equal stature. They include *Return to the River*, a novel about the great race of spring Chinook salmon that once populated the Columbia River, and his famous "season" series— *Fisherman's Winter, Fisherman's Spring, Fisherman's Summer,* and *Fisherman's Fall,* four of the most beautiful fishing books ever written.

Another writer who has given me almost as much satisfaction is Robert Traver, whose books *Trout Madness* and *Trout Magic* are among the most touching and amusing I have read. Traver writes exclusively of his passionate, whiskey-fueled pursuit of brook trout in the backwater ponds and creeks of Michigan's Upper Peninsula, and his books contain some of the funniest and most heartwarming tales in fishing literature. Traver is the pseudonym for John D. Voelker, a former justice of the Michigan Supreme Court who is better known as author of the best-selling novel *Anatomy of a Murder.*

Nick Lyons is another favorite. His books, *The Seasonable Angler, Fishing Widows,* and *Bright Rivers,* are written in a gentle, self-deprecating style with the sort of good-natured despair of an angler whose work has trapped him in the city and limited most of his fishing to daydreams; even on those rare occasions when he is able to get away, nothing ever seems to go quite right. Every angler who has experienced the frustration of being unable to go fishing, or of having something go wrong while he is fishing, will recognize something of himself in Lyons' tales.

Lyons also is a skilled editor who compiled one of the finest all-around collections of fishing stories ever published, an anthology titled *Fisherman's Bounty.* It would be hard to find another book capable of giving so much pleasure, but three other anthologies come very close—*In Trout Country,* compiled by Peter Corodimas; *Silent Seasons,* edited by Russell Chatham, and *The Ultimate Fishing Book,* with Lee Eisenberg and DeCourcy Taylor.

Chatham also is the author of *The Angler's Coast,* another well-crafted, entertaining book that never has received the attention it deserved. Other titles of equal merit are Ben Hur Lampman's *A Leaf from French Eddy*; Gingrich's *The Well-Tempered Angler* and *The Joys of Trout*; Edward Weeks' *Fresh Waters*; William Humphrey's *My Moby Dick* and *The Spawning Run*, and any book by Dana Lamb.

Where the Bright Waters Meet, by Harry Plunket-Greene; *A Summer on the Test*, by John Waller Hills, and *Thy Rod and Thy Creel*, by Odell Shepard, are three older classics that contain some of the finest lyric writing ever lavished on the sport. All three have recently been reissued and are available to the angling public for the first time in nearly two generations. Any one of them would be a solid cornerstone on which to build an angling library.

Bryan Curtis' *The Life Story of the Fish* is a book that deals more with appreciation for fish than for fishing, but it is so filled with sparkling insights and wry wisdom that any reader, even one not the least bit interested in fish, could scarcely fail to find it entertaining. Curtis was a respected scientist with well-honed literary instincts and this book displays both talents at their best; unfortunately, it is the only one he ever wrote. It too has recently been reissued.

Another unusual book is *Come Wade the River*, by Ralph Wahl, my friend and fishing mentor. For nearly half a century, Ralph has roamed the rivers of the Northwest with a camera in his vest, capturing the moods and scenes of angling more vividly than any writer ever could. Some of his best work is featured in this book, matched to some well-chosen words from *A River Never Sleeps*. The result is a stunning display of imagery and prose.

So far I have mentioned only titles which are still in print, recently reissued, or at least not so old they have grown difficult to find. There are others, dating all the way back to the 19th century or before, which are equally worth reading but are now nearly impossible to obtain.

One exception is a book that is more commonplace now than at any time during its 330-year history—Izaak Walton's *The Compleat Angler*, perhaps the most popular and enduring work ever penned in the English language. But it took a while for Walton's masterpiece to achieve such stature; shortly after it was published a London review damned it with the faint praise that it was "Not unworthy the perusall." Even today, revisionists attack some of Walton's prose as awkward and his literary devices as contrived, and we also know now that he copied shamelessly from the works of other writers—though such practice was rather more common and accepted in his time than it is in ours.

But whatever the revisionists may say, there is no denying that *The Compleat Angler* forever established angling as "the contemplative man's recreation" and made it a socially acceptable pastime for people of all stations. Any book capable of doing that had to be very special, and Walton's was—and is. It's also clear that whatever Walton may have borrowed from others he improved greatly by himself, and his prose evokes a spirit of serenity that has rarely been matched in all the centuries since. *The Compleat Angler* is a book every fisherman should read at least once in his life in order to fully comprehend the nature and meaning of his sport.

I have tried in this brief list to single out those books which have given me the greatest pleasure and fulfillment, those I believe would grace the shelves of any library and enlighten the mind of any fisherman. But regardless of which books an angler chooses to read, he will find the time it takes to read them is time not idly spent. In books he will share the excitement of the early discoveries of those who fished with horsehair lines and wrote by candlelight; he will fish alongside the masters, test their theories and take sides in the righteous fury of their great debates. Their rivers will become his rivers, their successes his to share, their traditions his to carry on.

All this and more is waiting, always waiting, just as often as one is willing to open the pages of a book.

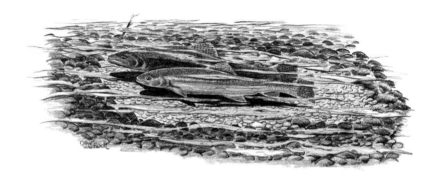

Steelhead Blues

If you go up to the headwaters in winter, you will see them: the survivors of the long return. They are steelhead, paired together in lonely pools or huddled on the redds, their bodies lean and dark and scarred from the stress of their upstream passage. They are a stirring sight, these great fish so far from the sea, so intent on fulfilling the purpose of their lives.

How far they have come! Perhaps from this very pool they began their long journey years before, following the river's flow blindly to the sea, riding the crest of the spring runoff down through the rapids and the pools until they felt the first lift of the rising tide. Then, following some ancient imprint of their race, they left the river to steer a secret course far across the sea, feeding and growing as they went, shedding the parr's bright paint for the silver gloss of ocean fish.

For two years or more they foraged in the trackless depths, growing fat and rich and strong. And then, one by one, each sensed a signal to return, a message from the past written in a genetic code a thousand generations old, and each responded to retrace its path homeward through the twilight of the sea, back to the river of its birth.

They found Indian nets and anglers' lures waiting in cruel welcome for their return and many fish were taken. Those which escaped faced an even greater test: A hard dash against the river's cold, full winter flow, with each fish spending its stored-up strength in a ceaseless struggle against the falling weight of December's rain and January's oozing snow.

Finally the survivors reached this place, this pool, somehow sensing it was right, and waited for nature to unfold the next step in the ancient drama of their race. And now at last they spawn, spilling their precious eggs into the gravel, committing them to the care of the river, trusting instinctively that in the fullness of time the river will bring forth life.

Days and weeks will pass and the raw winds of March will give way to the gentle rains of April. The snow on the higher slopes will begin its long retreat to the summits and the rivers will swell with its melt. The woods will brighten with the first fresh blush of spring and the tight red willow buds along the riverbanks will break; only then will the steelhead's progeny thrust themselves one by one from the gravel and into the light.

The adult fish never will see what they have bred. By the time the timorous alevins push out to begin their lives as fish, the surviving parents will be far again at sea, feeding on its riches, healing the wounds of their spawning and restoring the strength they spent against the river. And of those that do not survive the ordeal of spawning there will be no sign. The ragged remnants of their flesh long since will have been reclaimed by the ever-strict economy of the river, devoured by bird and beast and all the tiny teeming life of the stream, life which in its own turn will bring nourishment to the young steelhead emerging from the gravel.

For as long as man has walked the shores of the New World's rivers, the miracle of the steelhead has been played out before his eyes. At least some steelhead return in every month, but the greatest runs always have been in winter; yet even when the runs were still untouched by man, the steelhead always were much less numerous than the Pacific salmon with which they share so many rivers.

The salmon and steelhead were two of the most important reasons why Indians first settled in the Northwest and made their homes along its rivers. To the Indians, the primitive country must have seemed like a kind of rain-washed Garden of Eden—there were rivers full of fish, rich wild berry crops in summer, prairies filled with edible camas root, and forests of cedar from which to make longhouses and canoes. It was a place where Indians could live easily, and in time the river basins of western Washington became more densely populated with Indians than any other area north of Mexico.

Salmon were the mainstay of the Indians' life. They returned to the rivers at predictable times each year and the Indians knew this and waited to catch them. Five of the six Pacific salmon species are found in Northwest waters—the chinook, coho, sockeye, chum, and pink—and it seemed as if at least one of them was always running, from spring clear through to the early days of winter.

To most tribes, steelhead were less important simply because they were less numerous and because the largest runs came in winter when water and fishing conditions were often at their worst. But in some rivers, steelhead and salmon runs peaked together and the Indians caught them both, and the steelhead became nearly equal to the salmon in importance. And nearly every Indian fisherman knew that even when the rivers were empty of salmon, at least a few steelhead could probably be found.

The Indians fished with dip nets, crude gill nets, reef nets, spears, and cleverly constructed traps; they caught fish in weirs and impoundments, and they used trolling and jigging methods. They fished mostly in the estuaries and the rivers, but some ventured far out onto Puget Sound or onto the wild north Pacific Ocean. They learned not only the seasons but the locales in which the fish would run, and year after year they returned to the same fishing stations to await the returning salmon and steelhead.

Since salmon and steelhead played such vital roles in tribal life, it is hardly surprising that over time they took on a mystical, even religious significance to the tribes. Nearly every Indian group had its own version of the "first salmon" ceremony, a rite of celebration at the capture of the first salmon of the season. It included ceremonies whose purpose was to assure that the first fish would be the harbinger of a healthy run, and to remind tribal members they should do nothing to offend or waste this great natural gift that was so essential to their existence.

The Indians even saw salmon in the stars. Those who lived along the Nisqually River, south of the modern city of Tacoma, would watch by night as the constellation Orion ascended slowly in the autumn sky, knowing that when it reached a certain point the chum salmon, which they called Tl'hwai, would return to their river, and with it would come Skwowl, the steelhead. To them, the three stars in Orion's belt symbolized Indian fishermen drawing in schools of fish; the bright stars of the Pleiades cluster resembled a school of fish, and on clear nights, when the northern lights flickered on the far horizon, the Nisquallys thought it looked like a giant school of herring turning up their white bellies.

It was important to the Indians' philosophy never to take more fish than they needed in order not to offend the beneficent spirits who sent them. As long as that was their belief the runs remained healthy, for even at their peak the Indians never were numerous enough to have a significant impact on their size. For countless centuries the tribes lived in harmony with the salmon and steelhead, timing their travels to the migrations of the fish, carrying on the rituals they believed would assure their return, and tracing the shapes of salmon and steelhead among the stars. But late in the 18th century they began to feel the first touch of the outside world.

That touch seemed light enough at first, a series of brief encounters with strange white men who appeared off the coast on great sailing ships such as the Indians never before had seen. Sometimes these meetings led to bloody clashes, but more often they were peaceful and the sailors traded with the Indians for fish and pelts.

The white men always sailed away as mysteriously as they had come, but they left behind an invisible legacy of disease that spread rapidly among the tribes; lacking immunity, the Indians died in great numbers. Perhaps as many as half of all the Indians living in the Puget Sound area died in the period of early contact with the whites.

And then the white men began to come and stay—a few fur traders and trappers at first, then prospectors and speculators, finally settlers lured by a promise of unclaimed land and a dream of cities rising on the shores of Puget Sound. In the beginning there were not enough of them to have much effect on the Indians' way of life, for the land and its resources were large enough for both. The Indians continued fishing for themselves and increasingly were hired to fish also for the whites, and a mutually beneficial commerce grew up between them.

The settlers had little interest in the fishery, except for their own use. Their techniques for preserving fish were primitive, and since the Northwest was so far from the rest of the civilized world, shipments of steelhead and salmon spoiled long before they could arrive at market. In fact, Puget Sound salmon soon gained a bad reputation among the fish dealers of distant cities because it always was in such poor condition when it arrived, and this effectively discouraged any thoughts of a commercial fishing industry among the early settlers.

But the increasing settlement of the Northwest drew the government's attention to the potential value of the region and the United States negotiated a series of treaties to extinguish the conflicting claims of Spain, Russia, and Great Britain. Then, on August 14, 1848, Congress approved an act establishing the Oregon Territory, which included the present bounds of Washington state.

Five years later Washington was split off as a separate territory and Isaac Stevens was appointed governor. Stevens' instructions were to unite "the numerous bands and fragments of tribes," negotiate treaties with them, and furnish the government with a map showing the areas occupied by each tribe and the territories it claimed.

The notions of political structure and land ownership were foreign to the tribes, but Stevens set out to educate them on the rudiments of both. He appointed Col. Michael T. Simmons to visit the Puget Sound tribes, determine their numbers and the boundaries of the territories they claimed and try to organize them into political entities with which Stevens could negotiate. Stevens also enlisted the help of George Gibbs, a lawyer, surveyor, and ethnologist, and Col. B. F. Shaw, an interpreter, to help with the forthcoming negotiations.

After much preliminary work, Stevens and Gibbs compiled a census that showed 7,559 Indians were living in western Washington in 1854, although their count almost certainly was inaccurate and incomplete. The white population of the territory at the time has been estimated at about 2,000.

Stevens and his assistants also succeeded in dividing the Indians into discrete tribes and bands, simultaneously appointing many chiefs and subchiefs to represent their fellow tribesmen in negotiations. In one case, the Skopamish, Stkamish and Smulkamish Indians, which lived along the White and Green rivers a little east of Puget Sound, were combined into a group Stevens called the Dwamish, under a chief whose name the white men had difficulty both pronouncing and spelling. The name they finally settled on was Seattle.

Having made everything ready, Stevens scheduled a series of parlays with the tribes for the purpose of concluding the treaties. Among those invited to attend one of these meetings was the diarist James G. Swan.

"During the winter I received from Governor Stevens a letter inviting me to be present at a meeting to be held early in the spring on the Chehalis River, for the purpose of making a treaty with some of the Coast tribes relative to a purchase of their lands," Swan wrote. "This meeting was to take place at the clearing of a settler about ten miles from the mouth of the river, and the day designated was the 25th of February, 1855."

In the company of William B. Tappan, Indian subagent for the southwestern section of the territory, a certain "Dr. Cooper," and a contingent of local Indians, Swan left his home on Willapa Bay and traveled by canoe to the rendezvous site. "As we approached the camp we all stopped at a bend in the river, about three quarters of a mile distant, when all began to wash their faces, comb their hair, and put on their best clothes," Swan wrote. "The (Indian) women got out their bright shawls and dresses, and painted their faces with vermillion, or red ochre, and grease, and decked themselves out with their beads and trinkets, and in about ten minutes we were a gay-looking set; and certainly the appearance of the canoes filled with Indians dressed in their brightest colors was very picturesque, but I should have enjoyed it better had the weather been a little warmer. . . .

"Governor Stevens gave us a cordial welcome, and, after expressing the gratification he felt at the sight of so many canoes filled with well-dressed Indians, told us to go to the campfire, where he had ordered a breakfast to be ready for us, and we soon had a hearty meal of beefsteak, hot biscuits, and coffee, and were then shown the tent which had been assigned to us, where we proceeded to put ourselves to rights, and then took a look around to see the lay of the land.

"The campground was situated on a bluff bank of the river, on its south side, about ten miles from Gray's Harbor, on the claim of Mr. James Pilkington. A space of two or three acres had been cleared from logs and brushwood, which had been piled up so as to form an oblong square . . . In the centre of the square, and next to the river, was the governor's tent, and between it and the south side of the ground were the commissary's and other tents, all ranged in proper order. Rude tables, laid in open air, and a huge framework of poles, from which hung carcasses of beef, mutton, deer, elk, and salmon, with a cloud of wild geese, ducks, and other small game, gave evidence that the austerities of Lent were not to form any part of our services.

"Around the sides of the square were ranged the tents and wigwams of the Indians, each tribe having a space allotted to it. The Coast Indians were placed at the lower part of the camp; first the Chenooks, then the

Chehalis, Queniult and Quaitso, Satsop or Satchap, Upper Chehalis and Cowlitz. These different tribes had sent representatives to the council, and there were present about three hundred and fifty of them, and the best feelings prevailed among all." Only 14 white persons were present, including Stevens, Gibbs, Shaw, and Simmons.

"The next morning the council was commenced. The Indians were all drawn up in a large circle in front of the governor's tent and around a table on which were placed the articles of treaty and other papers . . . His excellency the governor was dressed in a red flannel shirt, dark frock-coat and pants, and these last tucked in his boots California fashion; a black felt hat, with, I think, a pipe stuck through the band, and a paper of fine-cut tobacco in his coat pocket. . . .

"After Col. Mike Simmons, the agent, and, as he has been termed, the Daniel Boone of the Territory, had marshaled the savages into order, an Indian interpreter was selected from each tribe to interpret the Jargon of Shaw into such language as their tribes could understand. The governor then made a speech, which was translated by Colonel Shaw into Jargon, and spoken to the Indians, in the same manner the good old elders of ancient times were accustomed to deacon out the hymns to the congregation. First the governor spoke a few words, then the colonel interpreted, then the Indians; so that this threefold repetition made it rather a lengthy operation. After this speech the Indians were dismissed till the following day, when the treaty was to be read.

"We were then requested by the governor to explain to those Indians we were acquainted with what he had said, and they seemed very well satisfied. The governor had purchased of Mr. Pilkington a large pile of potatoes, about a hundred bushels, and he told the Indians to help themselves. They made the heap grow small in a short time. . . .

"The second morning after our arrival the terms of the treaty were made known. This was read line by line by General Gibbs, and then interpreted by Colonel Shaw to the Indians." The treaty called for the tribes to cede their lands and agree to be placed on a reservation between Gray's Harbor and Cape Flattery. For this they were to be paid $40,000 in installments, plus $4,000 to enable them to "clear and fence in land and cultivate."

"No spiritous liquors were to be allowed on the reservation; and any Indian who should be guilty of drinking liquor would have his or her annuity withheld," Swan recorded. "Schools, carpenters' and blacksmiths' shops were to be furnished by the United States; also a saw-mill, agricultural implements, teachers, and a doctor. All their slaves were to be free, and none afterward to be bought or sold. The Indians, however, were not to be restricted to the reservation, but were to be allowed to procure their food as they had always done, and were at liberty at any time to leave the reservation to trade with or work for the whites.

"After this had all been interpreted to them, they were dismissed till the next day, in order that they might talk the matter over together, and have any part explained to them which they did not understand. The following morning the treaty was again read to them after a speech from the governor, but, although they seemed satisfied, they did not perfectly comprehend. The difficulty was in having so many different tribes to talk to at the same time, and being obliged to use the Jargon, which at best is but a poor medium of conveying intelligence. . . .

"Several of the chiefs spoke, some in Jargon and some in their own tribal language, which would be interpreted into Jargon by one of their people who was conversant with it; so that, what with this diversity of tongues, it was difficult to have the subject properly understood by all. But their speeches finally resulted in one and the same thing, which was that they felt proud to have the governor talk with them; they liked his proposition to buy their land, but they did not want to go on to the reservation.

"The speech of Narkarty, one of the Chenook chiefs, will convey the idea they all had. 'When you first began to speak,' he said to the governor, 'we did not understand you; it was all dark to us as the night; but now our hearts are enlightened, and what you say is clear to us as the sun. We are proud that our great father in Washington thinks of us. We are poor, and can see how much better off the white men are than we are. We are willing to sell our land, but we do not want to go away from our homes. Our fathers, and mothers, and ancestors are buried there, and by them we wish to bury our dead and be buried ourselves. We wish, therefore, each to have a place on our own land where we can live, and you may have the rest; but we can't go to the north among the other tribes. We are not friends, and if we went together we should fight, and soon we would all be killed.' This same idea was expressed by all, and repeated every day."

More Indians had come into camp and a census showed the number had grown to 843. "There were men among them possessed of shrewdness, sense, and great influence," Swan wrote. "We all reasoned with them to show the kind intentions of the governor, and how much better off they would be if they could content themselves to live in one community; and our appeals were not altogether in vain; several of the tribes consented, and were ready to sign the treaty; and of these the Queniults were the most prompt, evidently, however, from the fact that the proposed reservation included their land, and they would, consequently, remain at home.

"I think the governor would have eventually succeeded in inducing them all to sign had it not been for the son of Carcowan, the old Chehalis chief. This young savage, whose name is Tleyuk, and who was the recognized chief of his tribe, had obtained great influence among all the Coast Indians. He was very willing at first to sign the treaty, provided the governor would select *his* land for the reservation, and make him grand *Tyee*, or chief, over the whole five tribes; but when he found he could not effect his purpose, he changed his behavior, and we soon found his bad influence among the other Indians, and the meeting broke up that day with marked symptoms of dissatisfaction.

"This ill feeling was increased by old Carcowan, who smuggled some whisky into the camp, and made his appearance before the governor quite intoxicated. He was handed over to Provost-marshal Cushman, with orders to keep him quiet till he got sober. The governor was very much incensed at this breach of his orders, for he had expressly forbidden either whites or Indians bringing one drop of liquor into camp.

"The following day Tleyuk stated that he had no faith in anything the governor said, for he had been told that it was the intention of the United States government to put them all on board steamers, and send them away out of the country, and that the Americans were not their friends . . . That evening the governor called the chiefs into his tent, but to no purpose, for Tleyuk made some insolent remarks, and peremptorily refused to sign the treaty, and, with his people, refused to have anything to do with it. That night, in his camp, they behaved in a very disorderly manner, firing off guns, shouting, and making a great uproar."

The next morning, Governor Stevens called Tleyuk before the camp and gave him a severe reprimand, "and taking from him his paper which had been given to show that the government recognized him as chief, he tore it to pieces before the assemblage. Tleyuk felt this disgrace very keenly, but said nothing. The paper was to him of great importance, for they all look on a printed or written document as possessing some wonderful charm. The governor then informed that, as all would not sign the treaty, it was of no effect, and the camp was then broke up."

Tleyuk was not the only chief to defy Stevens, but the governor succeeded in getting most tribes and bands to sign treaties covering all of western Washington north of the Chehalis River. In each case the treaties were explained to the Indians in the crude Chinook Jargon, a trade language which had only a few hundred words—and no word at all for steelhead.

It seems doubtful the Indians ever had more than a general concept of the details of the treaties, but there is little doubt that each side in the negotiations knew what was foremost in the minds of the other. The white men wanted title to the Indians' land, and the Indians understood this; for their part, the Indians were determined to have continued access to the salmon and steelhead runs that had always sustained them, and the white men knew this. The whites also knew that if the treaties denied such access, there was no hope the Indians ever would agree to sign them.

Even so, Stevens and his associates might have made a bid to obtain some of the Indians' fishing rights if they had thought them worth very much; as it was, the Puget Sound salmon already had a poor reputation in the marketplace and seemed of little commercial value. In any case, the steelhead and salmon runs seemed limitless, and no one could foresee a day when there might not be enough for everyone. Allowing the Indians to keep their right of access to traditional fisheries therefore seemed a minor price for the whites to pay in return for the signatures they sought on the treaties, which would give them title to the Indian lands.

So a clause was written into the treaties to assure the tribes they would be able to continue fishing, and Governor Stevens was able to say to the Indians, as he did at the Point No Point Treaty council, "This paper secures your fish." The clause said that "the right of taking fish at usual and accustomed grounds and stations" was secured to the Indians "in common with all citizens of the Territory."

The treaties gave the whites what they wanted—title to the land— but they were not enough to avert bloodshed. Before the year 1855 was out, violence between Indians and whites had flared on both sides of the Cascades and an ugly little war was under way. It was a conflict that has all but escaped mention in history books, with the notable exception of the so-called "Battle of Seattle," but it continued well into the spring of 1856 in a series of nasty little skirmishes and ambushes in the woods and along the river bottoms south and east of Seattle.

Suffering and loss was heavy on both sides, but in the end triumph went to the whites with their superior weapons and firepower. Most survivors of the vanquished Indian bands were forced onto reservations, joining other tribes which had gone there peacefully after the treaties were signed.

Indians still outnumbered whites in the territory and at first, after things had settled down, most were able to leave the reservations and continue fishing at their traditional sites. The settlers offered encouragement by serving as a willing market for the Indian catch. The steelhead and salmon runs themselves apparently were as abundant as ever. The

Northwest still seemed far from the heart and nerve center of the nation, and in any case the country soon found itself totally preoccupied with the bloody conflict of the Civil War. Even Governor Stevens was caught up in the war's violent vortex, becoming a brigadier general in the Union Army. On September 1, 1862, near the country estate of Chantilly in northern Virginia, he snatched up a battle flag, led his men in a charge on Stonewall Jackson's lines and was shot dead. His sacrifice won him a small place in the history books, but for the next hundred years his role as the chief architect of the treaties was all but forgotten.

When the Civil War ended, a new wave of settlers came pushing westward and the white population of Washington Territory began to increase dramatically. The new arrivals claimed lands, cleared farms and built sawmills and towns, usurping some of the Indians' traditional fishing sites in the process. That was bad enough for the tribes, but a much more significant and subtle change also was taking place: Logging in the lowland valleys was beginning to strip the rivers and their tributaries of the shade that had kept them cool and comfortable for fish. Also, once the trees were gone, there was little to hold back runoff from the fall and winter rains; the rapid runoff eroded the soil and carried silt into streams where steelhead and salmon spawned. Enterprising farmers caused other problems, draining saltwater marshes and freshwater sloughs where young trout and salmon had sheltered and fed, converting them instead to croplands.

All these things were done without much thought for the fisheries, for the runs still seemed limitless; in any case, few people realized what consequences their actions ultimately might have upon fish or the rivers that sustained them.

Then a canning process was perfected that made it possible for the first time to ship salmon and steelhead to distant markets with assurance they would arrive in palatable shape. With this discovery, the fish runs suddenly took on enormous potential economic worth, and white fishermen moved swiftly to take advantage of it.

The first cannery on Puget Sound was built in 1877 at Mukilteo—ironically, the site where Chief Seattle and other Indians had signed one of Governor Stevens' treaties 22 years earlier. By 1894 the number of canneries had grown to three; by 1905 there were 24. The cannery fishermen borrowed a traditional Indian fishing method, the fish trap, and elbowed the Indians aside to stake their traps at sites where tribesmen had fished for countless generations. Once in place, the traps functioned with deadly efficiency on the returning runs.

At first there were no restrictions on the commercial fishery—no one ever had foreseen a day when restrictions would be needed—and whole runs were decimated or wiped out. After a few years of this, the decline in numbers of returning fish became so obvious that it was apparent something had to be done. Washington had become a state in 1889, and the next year the Legislature passed a measure that outlawed salmon fishing for three months of the year. Soon thereafter, the state began to require commercial fishermen to have licenses and started regulating the types of fish traps that could be used and their hours of operation. The Legislature also prohibited spearing, snagging, or snaring of fish.

Conservation was the motive for all these regulations, but they also had the practical effect of denying Indians access to the fishery and outlawing many of their traditional fishing methods. The tribes' original fear that they would lose the opportunity to fish was being realized.

Meanwhile, logging had grown into a major industry and many watersheds were stripped of their timber. After it was gone, tributaries used by salmon and steelhead for spawning began to flood in the spring and subside to low, warm flows in summer. Spawning beds were choked with silt, and logging slash formed barriers that kept fish from ascending streams. These drastic changes, coupled with the relentless pressure of the commercial fishery, reduced the runs from massive abundance to a shockingly low ebb in a few short years.

State authorities responded by authorizing construction of the first state salmon hatchery in 1895, beginning a long series of efforts to use hatcheries to overcome problems of damaged habitat and too much fishing pressure. In 1897 and again in 1899 the Legislature also approved additional conservation measures, ordering the closure of fishing in all tributaries and many estuaries of Puget Sound—once again denying the tribes access to some of their most valued salmon and steelhead fishing stations.

Despite the declining runs, the non-Indian commercial fishery continued to increase. Development of gasoline-powered engines allowed purse-seine vessels to venture into the outer waters of Puget Sound where they were able to intercept returning salmon in deep water long before other fishermen had a chance. Use of the highly efficient purse seines "stole upon us like a thief in the night," a state fish commissioner observed.

Engines also increased the mobility of gillnet boats, but the new technology actually reduced the overall efficiency of the fishery. Always before, mature salmon which had finished feeding and reached their peak weight and condition had been taken in river-mouth fisheries; now, seiners and gillnetters ranged far and took fish which had not yet reached their maximum size.

The Indians, mostly crowded onto reservations and living in poverty, lacked means to purchase boats and motors and join in this fishery, so they were left with a chance to fish only for those salmon which had been able to evade the outlying seines and gillnets.

By 1904, things were so bad that State Fisheries Commissioner T. R. Kershaw reported that "on Puget Sound the salmon have been steadily decreasing in numbers each year until even now the most optimistic concede that this industry will soon become one of comparatively little importance unless active steps . . . are taken." Steps were taken: more and more hatcheries were built, and more controls were imposed on fishing. But there were still no laws to protect against logging-caused erosion or pollution from the growing number of towns and mills on Puget Sound and its tributary rivers.

The steelhead runs, whose fate always has been inextricably intertwined with the salmon, suffered from the same problems. But although their numbers already had declined to a fraction of historical size, steelhead were beginning to win a small but dedicated following among sport fishermen. These were men who had discovered that the steelhead provided a rare quality of sport, enough to justify the effort of hiking or riding horseback to untrammeled upstream sites where it was still possible to fish the surviving runs.

For their part, the Indians seemed powerless to resist the changes that had taken away their right to fish as they always had. They were not even citizens of the country that had imposed itself on them, and thus had no representation on the councils that set fishing rules and regulations. They were also still widely regarded by the whites as little more than ignorant savages. As one early decision of the Washington State Supreme Court put it, "The Indian was a child, and a dangerous child, of nature, to be both protected and restrained. In his nomadic life he was to be left, so long as civilization did not demand his region. When it did demand that region, he was to be allotted a more confined area with permanent subsistence. These arrangements were but the announcement of our benevolence which, notwithstanding our frequent frailties, has been continuously displayed. Neither Rome nor sagacious Britain ever dealt more liberally with their subject races than we with these savage tribes, whom it was generally tempting and always easy to destroy and whom we have so often permitted to squander vast areas of fertile land before our eyes."

Considering a mind set like that, the Indians had little hope of obtaining relief in the state's courts. But federal courts were more friendly to their cause, and in one of the earliest fishing-rights cases, *United States versus Winans*, a white settler was ordered to remove four fish-wheel traps he had placed in the Columbia River at one of the Yakima Nation's traditional fishing places. In that 1905 case, the beginning of more than half a century of litigation, the U.S. Supreme Court observed that the Yakimas' right to fish at their accustomed places was "not much less necessary to the existence of the Indians than the atmosphere they breathed."

But even such words from the nation's highest tribunal were not enough to stem the tide running against the Indians. By the end of World War I, the non-Indian fishery had expanded to include a growing offshore troll fleet, which reached out beyond the seiners' territory to intercept returning fish at an even earlier stage in their migration. The salmon now had to run a triple gauntlet—the offshore trollers, the purse seiners and the inside gillnet fishery—before they reached the Indians' traditional estuarine and river fishing sites. By then their numbers had been so reduced that often there were barely enough remaining to meet spawning-escapement needs; Indians who tried to catch them were accused of trying to destroy the runs.

During the 1920s, the number of commercial fishermen increased faster than the catch and the average fisherman's income declined. The various fishing groups—trollers, seiners and gillnetters—squared off in bitter political contests to try to wrest a greater share of the rapidly declining resource for themselves.

Several other significant events occurred during that turbulent decade. On June 2, 1924, Congress passed an act that made every Indian a citizen of the United States. A year later, the Washington Legislature, responding to the rapidly growing popularity of the steelhead as a sport fish, declared that steelhead returning to fresh waters were to be classified as game fish and could not be taken in nets. At first this provision did not apply to steelhead in streams flowing across or next to Indian reservations, but two years later the Legislature eliminated that exception. Finally, in 1929, the Legislature also prohibited the commercial sale of steelhead.

The result of all these actions was to reserve the steelhead as a sport fish, protected from any kind of commercial fishery or exploitation. Aside from complying with the desires of sport fishermen, there were some very good economic and biological reasons for doing this, but as a practical matter it shut off still another traditional tribal fishery. The steelhead never had been as important as the salmon to most tribes, but the Legislature's move to close the steelhead fishery, coming as it did after the non-Indian commercial fishery had effectively usurped the salmon, was a bitter blow to the Indians.

But that wasn't the end. In 1935, state voters adopted an initiative prohibiting all "fixed-gear" fisheries. By this time, the Indians had few fishing sites left, and few were the salmon that returned to them, but the initiative made it illegal to use traditional trapping methods at these few remaining sites. It also closed inner Puget Sound to fishing by any means other than trolling or gillnetting, and the trollers and gillnetters quickly stepped in to take the fish Indians no longer were permitted to catch in traps.

Meanwhile, dams were beginning to add to the habitat problems already caused by logging, pollution, irrigation, and increasing industrial development in the Northwest. The Columbia River and its tributaries were hit hardest, beginning with completion of Rock Island Dam in 1933. That same year, making good on campaign promises, President Franklin D. Roosevelt commissioned a massive federal hydroelectric and irrigation development program on the Columbia, beginning with construction of Grand Coulee and Bonneville dams.

The Army Corps of Engineers' original design for Bonneville Dam contained no provision for fish passageways, which would have meant complete extermination of the Columbia's vast upriver salmon and steelhead runs, largest in the world. This was simply too much, and public protest finally forced the corps to reconsider and hire a team of biologists and engineers to design ladders to enable fish to ascend the 65-foot dam.

But Grand Coulee Dam would be 550 feet high, and there was no possible way fish ladders could be designed for a dam of that height; construction of Grand Coulee shut off the entire upper Columbia River Basin to migratory fish, blocking access to hundreds of miles of spawning water.

Over the years, dams proliferated on the Columbia and Snake rivers until they became a series of slackwater lakes behind stairstep barriers. Other dams were built on many of their tributaries, and west of the mountains many key rivers flowing into Puget Sound suffered a similar fate.

Both the state and federal governments continued to try to deal with these problems by building more hatcheries. Beginning in the early 1940s the Washington Department of Game, which was responsible for steelhead management, began propagating winter steelhead. But as often had been the case with salmon, little attention was paid to the origin of the stock used in these hatcheries. Steelhead from one river were trapped and spawned and their offspring were released in other rivers where they were expected to behave as if they were the progeny of natural runs that had returned to those rivers for thousands of years. Not surprisingly, they did not behave as expected, and those which managed to survive usually returned much earlier in winter than the native runs.

In a way this was good, for it spread the winter sport fishery over a longer time. Encouraged by these results, the Game Department began in the late 1940s to experiment with hatchery-reared summer steelhead. The first limited plants of these fish were made in lower Columbia River tributaries early in the 1950s and in 1956 a hatchery was completed to provide fish for a large-scale stocking program. By the early 1960s this program was under way.

Logging had been particularly harmful to the state's summer steelhead populations, destroying the cold, clear summer flows the fish needed to survive. The Game Department's stocking program succeeded in rebuilding some depleted runs and even created new ones in rivers which lacked them, most notably the Toutle River and its tributaries. Restoration of the steelhead runs provided great encouragement to anglers and the ranks of the state's license-holding steelhead fishermen swelled to several hundred thousand.

Meanwhile, intensive commercial net fisheries had developed in Alaskan and Canadian waters, intercepting Washington-bound salmon many hundreds of miles from their rivers of origin. Despite this increased competition, the number of commercial fishermen continued to grow and more hatcheries were built to pump out salmon in ever greater numbers.

All these things helped crowd the Indians into an ever smaller corner. Many Indians gave up fishing and left the reservations that always had been their homes, but a small cadre continued to eke out a bare subsistence on the tiny share of the resource that was left to them. Time and again they had appealed to friendly federal courts, and time and again the courts upheld their treaty rights with noble words that were largely ignored by state authorities, and nothing changed.

But in the 1960s Indians began to take notice of the growing success of the black civil-rights movement and decided to borrow some of its tactics. They began staging "protest" net fisheries for steelhead on the Puyallup River, challenging the state to intervene. A series of confrontations followed, some of them violent, and a number of Indians and their sympathizers went to jail. But these incidents drew widespread public attention to the fishing-rights issue, which was exactly what the Indians wanted.

Public attitudes had changed since the days when the state Supreme Court had called the Indian "a dangerous child" and the tribes found they had a great deal of sympathy from the majority of the white population not directly involved in fishing. Playing on these sympathies and the publicity generated by their protest fisheries, the tribes and their activist supporters began to bring pressure on the federal government to do something.

In September 1970, 115 years after the last treaty was signed, those efforts finally paid off when the United States, acting as trustee for seven western Washington Indian tribes, filed suit to enjoin the state from interfering with the fishing rights Governor Stevens had promised to the Indians. The case was assigned to U.S. District Judge George H. Boldt of Tacoma.

In many respects it was an unequal contest. After years as underdogs, the tribes suddenly had the full weight and resources of the federal government on their side. As additional tribes were allowed to intervene, their lawyers, together with those representing the federal government, grew to outnumber the state's attorneys by more than 10 to 1.

The state Departments of Fisheries and Game intervened as separate defendants in the case, but non-Indian sport and commercial fishermen had no direct voice in the proceedings. One reason may have been that they underestimated the importance of the case; after more than a half century of Indian fishing-rights litigation which had changed nothing, there was no apparent reason for them to believe this case might end differently.

The trial finally began on August 27, 1973, and continued for three weeks. Nearly 50 witnesses testified, including anthropologists, Indians, biologists, and fishermen, and the transcript ran to more than 4,600 pages. But when all was said and done, the issue boiled down to what Governor Stevens had meant when he told the Indians they had the right to fish "in common with all the citizens of the Territory."

On February 12, 1974, Judge Boldt ruled that "in common with" meant to share equally. In an historic opinion, the judge wrote: "It is the responsibility of all citizens to see that the terms of the Stevens treaties are carried out, so far as possible, in accordance with the meaning they were understood to have by the tribal representatives at the councils, and in a spirit which generously recognizes the full obligation of this nation to protect the interests of a dependent people . . . the mere passage of time has not eroded, and cannot erode, the rights guaranteed by solemn treaties that both sides pledged on their honor to uphold."

The essence of his ruling was that the treaties had reserved the Indians' right to fish, which meant that for non-Indians fishing was not a right but only a privilege. And Boldt departed from all earlier court decisions by quantifying the Indians' right; it meant, he said, that treaty fishermen were entitled to fish at their traditional off-reservation stations and catch half of all the returning salmon and steelhead not needed for spawning escapement. Non-Indians would have the opportunity to catch only those fish not needed to provide the Indians with their share, less whatever fish were necessary for spawning escapement. The tribes also were to become equal partners with the state in managing the fisheries.

The decision was a total victory for the tribes. Never before had their fishing rights been more than a vague legal concept; now they had firm meaning. And Boldt, a feisty and dedicated jurist, was determined to see that the meaning was enforced.

It took a while for the full impact of the decision to register on non-Indian fishermen. But then Boldt took control of the state's fisheries management, ordered early closures of the non-Indian commercial salmon fishery and sent state and federal agents to enforce his rulings, and suddenly the full meaning of his decision was clear to all.

It also was soon reflected in the catch statistics. In the years before the decision, the tribes had averaged only five percent of the area's salmon harvest; in 1974, after Boldt imposed restrictions on the non-Indian fishery, the tribal share increased to nearly 12 percent. Each following year saw more and more restrictions on the non-Indian fishery and a larger tribal catch.

The impact on steelhead was even more dramatic. In the three years before Boldt's ruling, the tribes' reservation net fisheries had taken about 23 percent of all the steelhead caught in the case area. In 1974 that figure jumped to 38 percent, in 1975 it surpassed 50 percent, and by 1976 it was nearly 66 percent. In some rivers, Indians caught nearly 100 percent of the harvestable steelhead run, leaving sport fishermen with nothing.

As these impacts became visible they stirred conflicts nearly as violent as the Indian war that had followed the signing of the treaties: Shots were exchanged, people were hurt, fishing boats were rammed, and angry sport and commercial fishermen marched in the streets and hung Judge Boldt in effigy.

Fate had played a cruel trick on the non-Indian fishermen. Most had fished all their lives, just as the Indians once had; for many, fishing had become a way of life, just as it once was for the Indians. Nearly all considered that fishing was their natural right, just as the tribes had once believed. Suddenly, through circumstances beyond their control, that right had been wrenched away from them, just as it had been taken from the Indians a hundred years before. And now they felt the same bitter hurt and blind frustration the Indians had felt in their darkest days.

Steelhead anglers were hit hardest by the ruling. Always before the Indian fishermen had been at the wrong end of a long funnel; now, with Indian nets strung across the mouths of nearly every steelhead river, it was the steelhead sport fisherman who suddenly found himself at the wrong end. The tribes concentrated on the winter runs, and soon the upstream reaches of the coastal rivers were lined with anglers waiting for fish that never came.

Angry though they were, the non-Indian commercial and sport fishermen seemed incapable of doing anything about their plight. Just as the Indians had been at the time of the treaties, non-Indian fishing groups were fragmented, disorganized, and at odds with one another, each group apparently unable to see beyond the limited horizon of its own selfish interests. They staged protests and wrote angry letters to editors and congressmen and cursed the Indians, Judge Boldt and one another, and some of them went to jail. But nothing happened.

Meanwhile, subsequent court decisions made matters even worse. Boldt's ruling was determined to apply not only to wild salmon and steelhead, but also to fish raised in state hatcheries; these were seen as replacements for wild stocks which had been depleted by the white man's careless treatment of their habitat. This meant that hatchery-reared steelhead, paid for by sportsmen's license fees, could be caught in Indian nets, a fact which further incensed steelhead anglers. A federal judge in Oregon also applied Boldt's 50-50 formula to the steelhead and salmon fisheries of the Columbia and Snake rivers.

In an ironic reversal of earlier history, many steelhead sport fishermen gave up fishing in disgust and many non-Indian commercial fishermen were forced out of business by the increasingly severe restrictions placed upon them; others fished in defiance of the regulations and went to jail for poaching.

In 1979 the U.S. Supreme Court upheld Boldt's ruling in nearly every important respect. After that the protests slowly sputtered out, the picket signs disappeared and in their place "For Sale" signs appeared on many fishing boats. Various legislative proposals or public initiatives to decommercialize steelhead were trotted out but most were beaten back, and these failures finally led some non-Indian fishing groups to belatedly conclude that compromise was their only hope—though they had little left with which to bargain. Meanwhile, federal promises of funds for fisheries enhancement went unfulfilled, and some fish runs, already endangered, declined even further.

For the Indians, the Boldt decision has meant greater self-esteem, a return of tribal members to the reservations, and a large increase in the number of Indian fishermen. Yet only a few members of the largest tribes have been able to make enough money from fishing to join the ranks of the middle class; most reservation families still have incomes far below their white counterparts.

The decision also revived many old prejudices that would have been better left forgotten. And by their actions in its aftermath, both sides have proved that prejudice and greed are not the exclusive traits of any race.

Despite the controversy, any careful reading of the Boldt decision or the long preceding record can hardly fail to lead a reasonable man to conclude that the decision was both morally and legally correct. But that is not to say it is without flaws; indeed, it has at least one very serious flaw, perhaps a fatal one: It requires biologists to predict run sizes and measure catches with a degree of precision that is impossible to meet—yet such precision is necessary in order to divide catches equally and assure enough fish are left for spawning. Judge Boldt failed to recognize that the chances for error in this approach are much greater than the chances for success, and any error that cuts into spawning escapement can very quickly bring a run of fish to the edge of extinction.

To be sure, Boldt's ruling has stimulated significant improvements in management techniques and knowledge, and this is all to the good; but it is unlikely that fisheries science ever will advance far enough to achieve the kind of absolute management precision that Boldt assumed was possible. That shortcoming, coupled with the fragmentation of management between federal, state, and tribal governments, could pose a grave danger to the future of the runs.

Beyond that, there is the larger question of whether it is wise social policy to divide the fish equally between a small number of Indians and the much larger community of non-Indian sport and commercial fishermen. As long as either side feels it is getting less than a fair shake, there is bound to be conflict, and this is a problem that ultimately must be resolved by the people rather than the courts. Unfortunately there is little sign that a solution is taking shape.

And so, from the early days of plenty, when the rivers ran full of fish and the Indians lived easily on their shores, we have come down to this: A divided society scrapping over the pitiful remnants of the once-mighty runs, arguing in court over who should be allowed to catch what little is left. It is, altogether, a sad story, a tale of greed, injustice, irony, and weakness on all sides, a tragedy for men and for fish—but especially for the fish.

If you really wish to understand it, then you must go up to the headwaters in winter and search for those scarred survivors of the long return. If you look long enough you will find them, paired together in the lonely pools or huddled on the redds. They are a stirring sight, these great fish so far from the sea, the last wild survivors of their kind. How far they have come!

If you see them, then you will know why men have followed them, worshipped them and fought so long and so hard for the right to fish for them.

And then, perhaps, you will truly understand.

Cutthroat Slough

Winter was hanging on like an old overcoat. It was the eve of April, but there was still no hint or sign of spring. Day after day the skies and the rivers were cold and gray. No flies hatched; no trout rose.

Faced with a restless urge to fish, I surveyed the limited prospects and decided to go in search of cutthroat. The cutthroat is a good fallback fish; no matter what the season or the weather, it seems there always are a few of them around. If you can find them, you can nearly always catch them.

A friend had told me about a slough where cutthroat sometimes were plentiful late in winter or early in the spring. Following a map, I drove to the spot, crossing a bridge over the outlet of the slough, then turning off on a pair of ruts that led across a farmer's frozen field. Beyond the field I could see the glint of water.

The road ended at the edge of the slough, near a ring of fire-blackened rocks that marked the remains of an old camp. Old maples grew along the water's edge, their winter-barren limbs leaning out over the slough like skeletal fingers. It was quiet there, and cold. The field behind the maples was deserted; there was not even a house in sight. But others had used the spot to camp, so I supposed it would be all right if I did so, too.

I was chilled by the time I had finished setting up my camp, manhandled my little aluminum pram down to the water and set up my rods. An icy wind scrawled changing patterns on the surface of the slough and the sky overhead was the color of slate, threatening snow.

The slough was wide near my camp, narrowing farther upstream until it disappeared among the trees. From the map I knew it was several miles long and I was near the lower end of it. It was actually the side channel of a great river, forming a giant arc from its upstream source until it emptied back into the main flow through the outlet I had crossed. Within the arc was a large island; my camp was on the island's edge.

The water was cold and dark with a slow current running through. The bottom, carpeted with the rotting remains of last year's leaves, sloped away quickly toward the far shore. It looked deep there, with a steep, moss-covered cliff dropping down to the water's edge.

I eased the little boat quietly into the channel and rowed within casting distance of the face of the cliff. There I began probing the deep water with a sinking line and a bright fly that was the only spot of color in the darkening day. Everything remained quiet. No birds sang, no insects hatched, no trout moved.

After a while thin tubes of ice began to form around my line, and I realized the air was growing even colder. The ice broke off and jammed in the rod guides so that after each few casts it was necessary to thrust the rod down into the water, which was only slightly warmer than the air, and leave it there long enough for the ice to melt away. Then I noticed a few flakes of snow were falling.

I had dressed warmly, but the cold had long since cut through my clothes and was toying with my bones. What was intended as enjoyment was rapidly becoming misery, and I was giving thought to quitting when a trout suddenly took hold. There was no warning; one moment the sinking line was slack, the next it was taut and throbbing with the feel of life on the other end. My numb fingers struggled for a grip upon the line as the graphite rod bent and bowed in cadence with the fish. The trout came to the surface and thrashed around, the first sign of life I had seen, and when it finally surrendered I led it to the side of the boat and saw with satisfaction that it was a bright cutthroat of a pound or better. I twisted the fly free and the fish quickly turned away and vanished in the dark water.

By then it was snowing harder, but the trout had revived my interest and I went on fishing. Soon I took another trout, a twin of the first, and then a third, smaller than the others. That was all for a while, but then I noticed a quiet dimple on the surface a little way upstream. Others followed, and it was obvious that several fish were feeding on the surface there. They were making quick, delicate rises, perhaps to the snowflakes that were striking the water in growing numbers.

I rowed within range of the rising fish and took up a rod equipped with a floating line and a small dry fly and began casting. The rises continued, but none came near my fly, so I replaced it with a small nymph and resumed fishing. Almost immediately the floating line gave a twitch and I raised the rod and set the hook in what turned out to be a feisty, plump whitefish—an unexpected bonus for what had started out as such an unpromising day. Moments later I hooked another, just as fat and feisty as the first.

I had grown so intent on fishing that I didn't see the canoe approach. It was less than a hundred feet away when I first noticed it, looming like a ghost through the gathering snow. It held two stern-looking Indians, their solemn eyes fixed steadily on me. Then I remembered from the map that the island where I'd camped was part of an Indian reservation—and I had not seen anyone to ask for permission to camp there, or to fish. The Indians did not look friendly; I wondered if there was going to be trouble.

The Indian in the bow of the canoe was short and stocky with a round face. His companion was tall and powerfully built, with long hair. Neither spoke nor changed expression as they drove the canoe closer with powerful paddle strokes. They came alongside, close enough to touch my boat, and then the short Indian suddenly grinned broadly.

"You shouldn't be out fishing on a day like this," he said. "It's too damn cold. Come ashore and we'll get you warm." Without waiting for an answer, he and his companion turned the canoe toward shore and quickly beached it. Within moments they had gathered wood and had a fire blazing.

I rowed ashore and beached my boat alongside the canoe and joined them at the fire. The smaller Indian reached inside his jacket and produced a bottle. "Here," he said, "this'll warm you up on the inside."

The fire was good and we passed the bottle back and forth while the smoke spiraled up into the thickening snow. The tall Indian sat and said nothing, and I never learned if he could speak. Perhaps he was one who followed the Old Ways and chose to speak only in a tongue I could not understand. But the other Indian—his name was Joey—more than made up for the silence of his friend. He was voluble and friendly and talked freely of fish and fishermen, of salmon and trout and their mysterious ways. He had seen few fly fishermen and knew little of the sport, but seemed fascinated when I opened up a box of flies and took some out and placed them in his hand. He was vastly pleased when I told him to choose a couple and stick them in his hat where they would always be handy for his use.

But he also was puzzled that I had come so far on such a cold day to fish only for cutthroat. "The cutthroat is such a small fish, he is not worth your time," Joey said. "You should come here later, in November, when the coho salmon are in and try to take them with your flies. I bet you could. I'd like to see you try." He made me promise that I would.

We talked on while the fire burned lower, the surrounding fields grew white and the nearby mountains disappeared behind a moving mist of snow. Soon there would be enough snow to make the roads difficult, possibly for days to come. I began to think better of my plan to spend the night.

Finally I said goodbye to Joey and his silent friend and left them by the fire. I rowed back to my short-lived camp, packed up, and drove away across the snowy field. Outside was an arctic scene, but inside my truck was warm and I felt good. I had caught some fish, and that was fine; but better yet, I felt I'd made a friend.

And I'd forgotten all about the long-delinquent spring. I was already looking forward to November.

Spring

Spring begins in March, a month named after Mars, the Roman god of war. And March is truly a month of conflict, a clash of seasons. Spring advances tentatively, then retreats before the last-ditch assaults of winter. Winter uses every weapon at its command, sneaking through the nights to leave killing layers of frost, or attacking boldly by day with knife-edged winds, lightning bolts, and bursts of rain or stinging hail.

Through the whole long month the battle rages, sometimes lasting well into April, which is supposed to be a peaceful month for planting. But despite the fury of the struggle, the outcome always is the same; the storms slowly lose their strength and ebb away, and spring presses forward to reclaim the barren battlefields of winter.

At first the signs are fitful, but then they come together all at once: Buds break open and leaves unfurl to catch the warming rain; mayflies come out to join the midges hatching on the lakes, and suddenly swallows and nighthawks are there among them. Trout and steelhead fry emerge from the river gravel, and soon the streams are filled with their quick, darting movements, masking the more cautious maneuvers of the older, wiser trout. At last the season has arrived; at last it is the time for which the trout fisherman awaits.

I remember going out on a spring morning after a long winter's wait to renew acquaintance with a river that February's floods had changed. The changes were many, but I was pleased to find one spot along the bank was still the same—a pleasant open patch of grass amid a growth of ferns. I stopped there to rest in the gentle warmth of the early afternoon and stretched out to watch the current flowing idly by.

Six weeks earlier the river had been gray and ugly and near flood, its surface swift and barren of any sign of life, its banks overhung with gaunt limbs that long ago had lost their last trace of foliage. Now the stream was clear and bright, with mayflies and midges dancing on the surface and trout rising eagerly to catch them; the trees were all in full green leaf, and everywhere there was color, sound, and movement. And I thought what a miracle it is that seasons can so swiftly pass and life so quickly reappear, and how spring is like a promise kept—especially for a trout fisherman.

A verse began to take shape in my mind and I reached inside my fishing vest and found a scrap of paper and an old blunt pencil and wrote it down. When I was finished I stuffed the paper back inside my vest, then returned to my fishing and soon forgot about it. Many seasons later I found the scrap of paper at the bottom of a pocket in my vest and wondered what it was. I took it out and unfolded it carefully; the paper was wrinkled, faded and yellowed by the years, but the words remained clear:

> Spring brings
> fulfillment
> of an angler's winter dream;
>
> A chance again
> to solve
> the silent silver secrets of the stream.

And now, each time winter sounds retreat and spring returns, I think again of those words—and give thanks once more for fulfillment of the dream.

Like Father, Like Son

Something magical happens the first time a father puts a fishing rod in his son's hand and leads him to trout water. It happened to me when I was five years old, going on six, and now I have seen it happen to my own son at the same age.

I hope he remembers it as well as I remember that first trip with my own father. It was a spring morning and the air had never been so clear. We followed a dirt road toward far mountains that stood out so vividly it seemed as if the horizon had been ripped along its edge. The road wound through pastures where white-faced Herefords grazed behind split-rail fences, then climbed into aspen groves and pine thickets where the ground still was wet with dew.

We came to a bridge over a small stream and my father stopped the car. The bridge was just a pair of heavy planks and the stream was hardly a stream; I could jump across it easily on my short, five-year-old legs. But it was filled with trout, which was the reason why my father stopped.

The trout had run up from a nearby lake and now they were spawning. Some of them were longer than the stream was wide and it was difficult for them to maneuver in the close quarters between the banks. But they went about their business purposefully, the females probing the gravel with their tails to prepare their nests while the males slashed and fought for the privilege of pairing with them. It was a fascinating sight, unlike anything I'd ever seen, and it prompted a feeling of awe and respect for trout that is with me still.

Later we drove on to Big Bar Lake, our destination, and spent the night in a log cabin on the shore. The next morning there was bright frost on the meadows and a thin layer of ice around the margins of the lake. Fire crackled in an old wood stove in the cabin and the sweet smell of alder smoke soon mingled with the odor of frying bacon. Breakfast was a hurried affair and then we rushed down to a leaning dock where a rowboat was waiting. My father took the oars and pushed off onto the still surface of the lake. When we were out far enough he took a fly rod, worked out the line, then placed the rod in my hand. "Hold tight, son, or the fish will take it from you," he warned.

We rowed slowly across the lake, and I held tightly to the handle of the long bamboo rod, trailing the sinking line behind the boat. The line slanted gently away into the depths and I wondered what was going on down there, and whether any trout could see the bright fly at the tip of the leader.

Soon enough one did, and the rod suddenly came alive in my little hand, throbbing with a strong, electric pull. Instinctively I thrust it back at my father, who took it and played the fish to the side of the boat. It was a foot-long trout, all bright and gleaming silver and quite unlike the dark and ruddy fish I had seen spawning in the stream. And it was a small matter that my father had landed it; I had hooked it, so it was "my" fish, and I proudly proclaimed it so while Dad grinned from ear to ear.

My father and I fished together many times thereafter, but never quite as often as we would have liked. He was an Army officer, a career that left few opportunities for fishing, so the opportunities took on added importance when they came. Always there were elaborate preparations—

food to be bought, sleeping bags and bedding to be aired and packed, fresh flies and leaders to be purchased, maps to be studied, plans to be made. But my favorite time was when we took the tackle out to see what things needed to be repaired or replaced.

Each item had its own special feel and scent. The reels were cold and solid to the touch and held braided silk lines with a strong aroma of linseed oil and silicon dressing. The bamboo rods had a musty scent mixed with a lingering odor of varnish, and the long brown shafts felt smooth and strong. We would join the sections together to test the fit, then flex the rods in the air and imagine them bending under the weight of a heavy fish. The fly boxes held a kaleidoscope of colors and textures and the names of the patterns were nearly as exciting and colorful as the flies themselves—Colonel Carey, Black O'Lindsay, Alexander, Nation's Special, Cummings Fancy, Rhodes' Favorite, Lioness, and others whose names escape me now.

Finally, when all was ready, we would pack the car the night before departure, and I would toss and turn in bed and be up well before the dawn, waiting impatiently until it was time to go. Usually my mother or one of my uncles or a fishing companion of Dad's would come along.

But on the last trip it was just the two of us alone. We didn't know, of course, that it would be our last trip together. We set out with the usual bright hopes, and Dad wore the happy look he always had when going fishing. It was not the best fishing we ever had, but neither was it bad, and on the last day we fished into the twilight in a driving rain until both of us were soaked. My father was shivering when we started back to camp, and by the time we reached it he was trembling uncontrollably. I built a fire, wrapped him in a blanket and made some soup and gave him some. After a while he seemed all right again, but it was the first time I had ever really worried about him.

I was 17 then and just about to start college, and back in Washington, D.C., they were cutting orders that would take my father to Germany. We saw each other only a few times after that, and there was never enough time for fishing. And then he suffered the heart attack that killed him.

Now his old reel sits atop my bookcase, the pungent smell of oil and dressing having long since faded. His old bamboo rod stands in its case in the corner, the luster long gone from its varnish. His old flies are carefully put away, but their colors, too, have faded over time.

But the memories remain—recollections of sunlit days and days of rain, of full creels and empty ones, of misty mornings full of promise and evenings spent cleaning a catch by lantern light. Remembered too are his lessons about what knots to tie, how to gauge the wind and light, and where to place the fly. But the brightest memory and the best lesson was one he taught subtly, a little at a time. Call it an attitude or feeling, a sort of inner excitement that returns each spring when the green buds burst open on the trees, the mayflies hatch, and trout begin to rise. It's that and more—a kind of understanding and appreciation that fishing is one of the very best things that ever a man can do, and trout fishing is the very best of all. It is one of my father's most precious gifts to me, and now I hope somehow to impart the same feelings to my son.

His name is Randy, the same as his grandfather whom he never had a chance to know. He is a strong and sturdy boy with a quick mind and many interests, of which fishing is one. It is not something that he has ever been compelled to do, nor has he ever been told that he should want to do it. It has been offered to him as an opportunity that is available whenever he wishes to take advantage of it. And often enough, he has.

The first time was at Dry Falls Lake. It was a spring morning, but a very different one from the long-ago day when I "caught" my own first trout. The sky was dark and streaked with lightning, the wind was cold and strong, and rain came in hard bursts. Randy was bundled up in heavy clothing that made it difficult for him to move, but he was at my side when I hooked a husky little trout and passed the rod to him. He squealed with delight when the fish jumped, then cranked the reel so furiously he nearly wound the fish up to the top guide of the rod before I could stop him. It was a proud moment for him, but an even prouder one for me.

Not long after that he asked if he could have his own rod, and I gave him one my father had given me, along with an old reel and a line. Soon he asked to learn to cast, and I have tried to show him how—sometimes to our mutual consternation, but sometimes, when all goes well, to our mutual delight.

Watching me tie flies one night, he asked to be shown the secrets of that art. Now, with a little instruction, a hand-me-down vise and hand-me-down materials, he is tying his own, which get a little better all the time. He has yet to take a trout on a fly he tied himself, but surely that day is not far off.

Some years ago we bought an old cabin on the North Fork of the Stillaguamish River, and when Randy watched me wade the stream he asked to follow suit. Not yet, I said; you're not quite old enough for that, and besides you have no boots or waders. But then a friend gave him a pair of children's-sized hip boots, and I no longer had a good excuse.

So on a summer day I helped him into the boots and strapped them to his belt. Even though they were children's size, the boots were too long for his short legs and they hung loosely in accordian pleats. Undaunted, he walked with me down to the river, and I showed him how to slide his feet over the slippery rocks, how to plant one foot firmly before moving the other, and how always to keep his body turned sideways to the flow. Then he put his warm little hand in mine and held tightly as we started out across a side channel to a small island. We reached it safely, waded back, then crossed again. In all, we waded the channel six times before Randy decided he had finally had enough. "Dad, I think that was the funnest thing I ever did," he said.

I thought it was one of the funnest things I'd ever done, too.

Each of these things has pleased me, as my own childhood fishing exploits must have pleased my father. But what a boy does is not always an indication of what he will do when he becomes a man, and there have been times when I have wondered if Randy's interest in fishing is a permanent thing or merely a passing fancy.

And then, last year, I think I got my answer.

Randy was eight then, and decided for the first time to go fishing by himself. He donned the hip boots—they fit a little better now—put his rod together, attached the reel, and threaded the fly line through the guides. He chose a fly without asking my advice, knotted it to the end of his leader, walked down to the river and waded alone into the same side channel we had crossed together a couple of years before. He found a spot to his liking, worked out line and began to cast, while his mother and I settled down to watch from among the trees on the high bank above the river.

Soon we heard his shout and saw the rod bend in a pulsing bow.

I saw the look of joy upon his face, and understood.

"He's hooked one," his mother said.

"No," I told her. "I think maybe it's the other way around."

The Dawn Trout

The St. Maries River is a placid little stream that follows a meandering course through a peaceful valley in the hills of northern Idaho. In most respects it seems an unremarkable little river, but there is much more to the St. Maries than meets the casual eye.

It is, for one thing, a very old river. The weathered ridges that define the limits of its valley once were shoals in a Precambrian sea, and they have shaped the flow of water through the valley since the world was young. For millions of years the river has carried the runoff from these hills, twisting and turning in its channel but always bearing northwest-

ward in the direction dictated by its confining ridges. The Pacific Northwest has hundreds of rivers of greater volume or personality or consequence, but few as old as this one.

You would not think it so old to look upon it now. In the early spring
its valley still seems fresh and new, with creeks running full and grass
growing tall and clots of winter snow lingering in the shaded hollows. Fat
cattle and handsome Appaloosa ponies graze in meadows along the river,
and columns of woodsmoke rise into the morning air from the little
settlement of Clarkia, a cluster of neat houses built on potholed streets
with logging rigs parked out in back. The rigs are there because of the
white pine, fir, cedar and hemlock that grow in the hills.

Below Clarkia, where Emerald Creek comes down from the hills to
meet the St. Maries, dredges churn the creek sediments to recover garnet
sand, but the dredge spoils are dumped in holding ponds so that both the
creek and the river still run clear. Above the dredging on Emerald Creek,
you can find caddis larvae with cases made of garnets, looking like little
living jewels as they crawl slowly and awkwardly among the rocks and
debris on the streambottom.

The logging and dredging provide most of the local jobs, but there
are not very many of either, and the valley remains sparsely settled. It is far
from any major highway or any city of consequence, and far from all the
problems that highways and cities bring. Its life is measured and orderly,
its rituals defined by the seasons, and its people are accustomed to hard
work and hard play. Their recreation reflects their attitude and spirit:
They like to race snowmobiles in the winter and trailbikes in the spring
and summer. And strangely enough, it was this interest in racing that led
to the discovery of some of the secrets hidden in the St. Maries' ancient
past.

It began with a man named Francis Kienbaum, who owned property near Clarkia and was well aware of the local interest in racing.
Kienbaum had an idea that a commercial racetrack might be a profitable
enterprise, and his own land seemed an ideal site; it lay in a hollow
between a pair of wooded knolls and was just the right size and shape for a
track. All that was needed was a little fill dirt to build up the turns of the
track, and there was plenty of dirt for the taking in the knolls at either end
of his property. A bulldozer could move it quickly and easily where it was
needed.

Having made these plans, Kienbaum decided one day in 1971 to
carry them out. He climbed into the cab of a bulldozer and began slicing
into the base of one of the knolls, cutting away the topsoil and pushing it

toward what would be the north turn of the track. On the first day he worked through the afternoon and into the evening and finally ran the bulldozer far into the night, digging ever deeper into the face of the slope.

But Kienbaum was scarcely prepared for what he found when he returned to the site next morning. What had not been visible in the darkness of the night before was revealed clearly in the morning light: His bulldozer had cut through the topsoil into a layer of soft clay, and the clay had broken up to reveal thousands of fossil leaves. And these were not ordinary fossils; to Kienbaum's astonishment, the leaves appeared to be intact and perfectly preserved. As he watched, some began to dry out, curl up and lift off the clay. One by one, they peeled off and were carried away by the morning breeze.

Kienbaum tried cutting into the clay with a knife and found that it split easily into thin layers like a pastry, with each layer containing more fossils. He found leaves that still wore green, red and golden colors from the springs and autumns of ages past, and again as he watched they dried out quickly, their colors faded, and the leaves curled up and blew away. He opened another layer of clay and this time found what appeared to be the fossil remains of a small fish.

Certain by now he had found something important, Kienbaum decided to report it to someone who could evaluate it properly. He made a telephone call to the University of Idaho in Moscow, 55 miles away, and ended up talking to a secretary at the College of Mines and Earth Resources. She jotted down the details of his story and gave the message to Charles J. (Jack) Smiley, a geology professor and a specialist in the arcane science of paleoecology, the study of prehistoric ecosystems.

Smiley is a wiry, energetic man with a powerful intellect and the kind of strong, innate curiosity that leads a man into science. He also is a man of omnivorous interests, and such a broad range is practically essential in the study of paleoecology. A paleoecologist is like a detective following a very cold trail—a trail that may be 20 million, 50 million, even 100 million years old or more. Even the very smallest clues—fossil flecks of pollen or tiny spores—may have meaning to such a scientist, and his work requires the utmost patience and perseverence in evaluating every detail.

So when Smiley received the message, he was anxious to see what Kienbaum had found. Early the next morning, he drove to the racetrack and quickly confirmed that Kienbaum had made a major discovery—a treasure trove of unusually well-preserved fossil leaves and fish. Subsequent analysis would show them to be from the Miocene Epoch; in other words, the leaves turned up by Kienbaum's bulldozer and carried off by the morning breeze had last known the light of morning nearly 20 million years before.

Kienbaum's find would provide Smiley and others with much work in years to come—the work of taking, preserving, and classifying samples, of analyzing and interpreting them, then finally of translating all the results into a written record to become a permanent part of the published knowledge of earth's past. In the process of this work, a picture of the prehistoric St. Maries valley began to emerge:

Sometime during the Miocene Epoch, a tongue of molten magma had forced its way up through a fissure in the ancient rock that bounded the St. Maries and spilled out onto the surface as a lava flow. The lava had hardened into a dam that blocked the river, causing the valley to fill with water and form a lake nearly 25 miles long. Smiley and Bill Rember, a graduate student who assisted in the research, named it Miocene Clarkia Lake.

The Cascade Mountains had yet to rise when the lake was formed, and northern Idaho was near the eastern edge of a plain that extended almost unbroken to the Pacific Coast. The climate was much warmer and more humid than it is now, and the fossil evidence showed that swamp cypress, water lilies, and cattails had grown up around the shoreline of the lake. On the lower slopes of the surrounding hills were stands of oak, maple, sycamore, sweetgum, tulip trees, magnolia, and other plants now commonly found in forests of the southeastern United States, but long gone from the Idaho hills. Coniferous trees grew on the higher, cooler slopes above the lake, and all the plants shed their leaves and seeds and pollen to the wind, which carried them out over the open water. There they had fallen to the surface and sunk slowly to the soft muck of the bottom, where they were joined by the remains of beetles, bugs, caddis-flies, ants, and other insects that also had fallen into the water, and by the remains of sunfish, minnows, and other aquatic organisms from the lake itself.

The fish had lived near the wind-stirred surface of the lake, above a thermocline that protected a layer of cold, stagnant water near the bottom. It was in this bottom layer where all the plant and animal remains came finally to rest, where each in turn had been covered by a slow rain of silt washed in from tributary streams, or by great falls of ash carried on the wind from distant volcanoes. The lake bottom was a static, sterile environment, so lacking in oxygen that there was no decay. And that is why leaf tissues still wore their colors when Kienbaum's bulldozer sliced into the knoll so many millions of years later; few other sites in the world have yielded fossils preserved so perfectly as those from Miocene Clarkia Lake.

The site of Kienbaum's racetrack, which he promptly named the "Fossil Bowl," once had been a small bay near the upper end of the lake. Surveys disclosed other fossil deposits in the valley, but none as rich as the racetrack site; a layer-by-layer analysis of a thin column of lake-bottom clay from the racetrack yielded a count of more than 10,500 plant fossils.

Despite the richness of its fossil deposits, the lifespan of Miocene Clarkia Lake was hardly more than a mere flickering instant on the grand scale of geologic time. Ash and silt accumulating on the bottom filled the lake so that its outlet cut an ever-deeper channel through the lava dam. Without the dam to hold it back, the lake quickly disappeared, and once again there was only a placid little river flowing through the long valley. The lake had been born and had lived and died in less than a thousand years, and when it was gone there was hardly any evidence that it had ever existed—except for the fossils that would remain hidden for so long.

In the years immediately following Kienbaum's discovery, the ancient lake gave up its secrets generously, including some that were new to science. Among its fossil fish was a new species, *Archoplites clarki*, a sunfish that may have been a predator with habits similar to those of the modern bass. Among its fossil leaves and fruit were specimens that Smiley classified as a previously unknown genus, *Pseudofagus*, an extinct relative of today's beech trees. And there were many other matters of scientific interest.

But Miocene Clarkia Lake still had one more surprise in store, and nine years would pass before it came to light.

The morning of June 12, 1980, was warm and still with a threat of thunder in the air. Mount St. Helens had erupted less than a month before, and a fresh layer of powdery volcanic ash lay upon the earth exposed by nine years of digging when Smiley, Rember, and two other students arrived at the racetrack site to begin searching for more plant fossils. They had been at their work only a short time when Rember thrust his knife into a piece of clay, split it open and found himself staring at what appeared to be the bones of a fish—one much larger than any ever found before. Rember thought it might be the remains of a gar, a primitive freshwater fish whose descendants still live in the eastern and southern United States. He shouted and the others came running.

Excited by the size of the find, they began working carefully to lift up other pieces of the clay that concealed the rest of the fossil. It was ticklish work; the fossil was imbedded in a layer of clay only half an inch thick, already fractured in places, and below it was a layer of ancient volcanic ash from which the clay could easily separate and fall. Slowly they exposed more and more of the fossil, but by lunchtime the task still was not finished. The foursome covered the fossil with a plastic sheet and drove to a cafe in nearby Clarkia.

The thunderstorm struck while they were at lunch, and by the time they returned to the fossil site the diggings had turned to sticky mud and water was rushing down the slope. Despite the downpour and the uncomfortable conditions, they resumed work until finally the full outline of the fossil was revealed—not that of a gar, but of a large, distinctly trout-like fish. The fish was complete except for a few parts of the skull; even its lateral line was still evident.

The fossil was removed in several pieces, wrapped in newspaper and placed in a box for transportation back to the geology laboratory at the University of Idaho. When the pieces were reassembled at the laboratory, the fish was measured at a length of 72 centimeters, or slightly more than 28 inches. Then the still-wet pieces of thin clay, reassembled in their original shape, were placed in a press and left there to dry out and to harden and compress the clay.

After five weeks the fossil finally was dry and work began to try to identify what kind of fish it was. All the other fish fossils unearthed from Miocene Clarkia Lake had belonged to the sunfish or minnow families, and none had measured more than eight inches long; this one was clearly something quite different.

Smiley and Rember photographed the fossil and sent slides and prints to Dr. Gerald R. Smith of the University of Michigan Museum of Paleontology, an expert on the taxonomy of early fish. Smith sent a graduate student to retrieve the fossil and carry it from Moscow back to Michigan where he could study it in person.

Smith's verdict was that the fossil was that of a "large trout" with characteristics "unlike any other genus of North American salmonid." Its jaws and teeth were too large for it to have been a grayling; it had too few vertebrae, scales and anal-fin rays to have been a Pacific salmon; its scales and vertebrae were larger than those of any existing North American trout, and its dorsal fin had more rays than any char. But if it was not any of those things, then what was it?

Smith concluded that there *was* one fish which shared all the characteristics of the fossil trout: The *Hucho*, a Eurasian salmonid commonly known as the Huchen. The Huchen, which bears a superficial resemblance to the Atlantic salmon, today is found in the Danube Basin of southern Europe, Siberia, and waters of the Far East, and in some of those areas it is prized as a sport fish.

But the identification raised a major question: The Huchen has not been known on the North American continent within the history of man's occupation; if the Clarkia Lake fish really was a Huchen, then where could it have come from?

Smith proposed an answer for that, too. He theorized that millions of years ago, when the Bering Land Bridge was in place between Siberia and Alaska and the Bering Strait was closed, there was a free interchange of fish between North America and Asia. Sometime during that period, the Huchen may have migrated from Asia and found a hospitable home in the prehistoric lakes of the Northwest, where the climate was moist and mild. Or, conceivably, it might have been the other way around—the Huchen could have evolved here first and emigrated to Asian waters.

Wherever it came from, there was other circumstantial evidence to support the identification of the Miocene Clarkia fish as *Hucho*. Earlier fossil finds in sediments of prehistoric Lake Idaho on the Snake River Plain also closely resembled Huchen, although these fish were perhaps 10 million to 15 million years younger than the Clarkia Lake fish.

Still, Smith labeled his identification of the Clarkia fish "preliminary." He has suggested the fish may have been an intermediate, ancestral evolutionary line that led to the modern Huchen and the modern chars, and although he believes his identification of the fish as *Hucho* is "pretty solid," there is always the chance that future discoveries might show it was part of a line that led to the chars. If that happened, the Clarkia Lake fish might have to be reclassified.

At approximately 20 million years, the Miocene Clarkia fish is the second oldest salmonid fossil ever found. The oldest, at 40 million years, is *Eosalmo driftwoodensis*, described in 1977 from the Middle Eocene Driftwood Creek fossil beds near Smithers, British Columbia. Bone fragments and scales of even older fish have been found, but the type specimen of *Eosalmo* was nearly intact.

Compared with the Clarkia fish, *Eosalmo* was small, about 11½ inches long, with features intermediate between those of the grayling family and the Salmoninae—the Huchen, chars and trouts. But Smith reported no indication of a lineage from *Eosalmo* to the Clarkia fish, or to the still younger fossils from the Snake River Plain. Nor was the Clarkia fish apparently the ancestor of any living North American salmonids. "Its relationships seem to be with Eurasian forms," Smith wrote.

So the Huchen apparently ran its course in North America for several million years, then vanished. Why did it disappear? Again, there are only theories: Perhaps it lost out in competition with separately evolving chars and trout, or perhaps it was a victim of a change in the climate that began about 2 million years ago when the first of successive waves of glaciers swept down over the roof of the continent. No fossil remains of *Hucho* have been found from after that time.

Whatever the reason, when the first men arrived to begin exploring the rivers and lakes of North America, they found Pacific salmon, trout and char in abundance, but no trace of Huchen. Its former presence here was never guessed or imagined until its fossilized remains were unearthed so many years later. And even now, after those remains have been studied and identified, the idea that Huchen once lived in our lakes and traveled our rivers is so remote that it almost seems an abstraction.

But there is nothing abstract about the fossil fish of Miocene Clarkia Lake. Once it was a living creature, with instincts and purpose; it sought food and fled danger and perhaps rolled in the evening twilight even as large trout do in the twilights of our time.

Perhaps it was the offspring of a race of fish that had ranged far across a prehistoric sea and found their way into the rivers of a new continent, with each generation working farther inland along a network of rivers and lakes far too old for any human to remember. Perhaps it had traveled far itself, spending its life in a compulsive urge to press forward and see what lay beyond the next bend of the river—until one day, after rounding hundreds of bends in scores of rivers, it came finally to the foot of a heavy flow spilling from a lava dam that held back a lake high in the hills. The falls would have been a formidable obstacle, and it may have taken the fish many tries to clear them, but eventually it did, and its reward was a chance to rest in the quiet waters of the lake.

But its rest would have been brief, for a new compulsion would have hurried the fish along through the lake to the mouth of a small tributary rushing down the slopes of a ridge that once was a shoal in a Precambrian sea—perhaps a tributary where caddis larvae crawled on the bottom and made their cases of tiny garnets plucked from the sand. And in that little tributary, the fish might have found another of its kind, a veteran of the same long journey; and there, in a quiet pool under the protective shade of sweetgum and magnolia trees, the two of them would have made a redd and filled it with their spawn.

After that the end would have come swiftly for the fish. Having spent its last energy in spawning, it could not long resist the tributary's flow; the current would have swept it downstream, tumbling and drifting until it was back in the quiet waters of the lake. Even those restful waters would not have been enough to restore its strength, and finally, in a little bay near the lake's upper end, it would have settled slowly down into the cold, dark water and the silt, joining the day's harvest of fallen leaves and insects. And there it would remain until a warm spring morning with a threat of thunder in the air, 20 million years later.

A fanciful tale? Perhaps. But if we could ever learn the full story of the fossil fish of Miocene Clarkia Lake, it might not be so very different. Possibly one day we shall know more: Chemical analysis of the fossil may yet reveal more of its life's history.

Meanwhile, the valley of the St. Maries remains a sleepy, peaceful place, little changed by its scientific notoriety. Except for the "Fossil Bowl" sign on Kienbaum's racetrack, there is not much to suggest the area's ancient heritage.

But if you should go there in the spring, when the camas lily is blooming in the meadows near the river, you might see a reminder of the past: Stand on a high hillside and look down at the fields of waving blue blossoms and it will seem very much as if you are looking out upon a sparkling lake—like one that filled the valley 20 million springs ago.

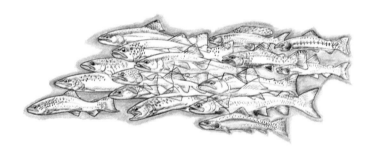

Family Tree

Man's unending search for the origins of life has impelled him to look from the deepest seas to the most distant corners of the universe, and far back to the very beginning moments of time. He is understandably most curious about his own origins, but he has not neglected the other forms of life with which he shares his world—including trout.

Yet in many ways, searching for the trout's lineage is even more difficult and demanding than searching for our own. One reason is that the quest for early man is a more glamorous undertaking and therefore commands more attention, time and money; another is that the trout's span of history is much greater than our own, and so it is necessary to search much farther back in time for its origins. Early man also left more for us to find; besides his own remains, he left primitive tools and spearpoints, the campfire middens of his dwellings, and galleries of enigmatic artwork painted on the walls of ancient caves. The trout left us only its bones.

Even when we are lucky enough to find some of those bones, it sometimes only makes matters more complicated. The story of the fossil fish of Miocene Clarkia Lake is a case in point: Here were the remains of a fish long extinct in North America, found where no one really expected them to be. Finding them did not simplify the effort to trace the evolutionary lineage of trout; instead, it merely forced scientists to come up with an explanation for how a fish previously thought native only to Europe and Asia could have been living in northern Idaho 20 million years ago.

But even if they present new problems, such fossil finds always are valuable because they offer a snapshot of how matters stood on the evolutionary scale at a particular time and place. They also are the best evidence we have of things gone before, key parts in a giant jigsaw puzzle from which most of the pieces are still missing.

Other evidence may be obtained by examining the distribution and genetic relationships of living trout, but here again there are complications. The problem is that trout and their kindred species still are dividing themselves up into separate forms, so that it becomes necessary for scientists to try to determine the point of their last division, plus the one before that, and all the other ones before that, in order to figure out where they came from and how they got to be the way they are.

Scientists have employed a formidable arsenal of weapons in an effort to solve these problems and trace the trout's lineage back to a common ancestor, or at least a group of ancestors. These include such sophisticated modern techniques as electrophoresis, an electrochemical means of measuring genetic similarities among living fish; complex studies of comparative anatomy, and computer methods for discerning relationships among fish. But they also still include the sweaty, unsophisticated work of swinging a pick against a hard surface of sun-baked clay or rock to get at the fossils presumed to lie underneath.

These methods, and the hard work of the men and women who wield them, have led to a theory of how trout evolved. It does not attempt to say precisely when or exactly where the first trout-like fish appeared, nor does it seem likely that any theory ever shall be able to say so with very much certainty. Neither is it a finished theory; like the trout itself, it continues to evolve. And not all of its elements are unanimously accepted; some remain in hot dispute. Yet for all that, it is the best explanation we now have.

It supposes that the lineage of trout extends back at least as far as the late Cretaceous period, about 100 million years ago. The seas of that time held fish belonging to an order that men much later would call the Salmoniformes, a diverse group whose modern members include the freshwater pikes and mudminnows and marine forms such as the strange deepsea bristlemouth, the spookfish, viperfish, and deepsea dragonfish.

Sometime within the late Cretaceous period there occurred a "polyploid event," a doubling of chromosome numbers and DNA in an ancestral species that caused it to diverge from the evolutionary path of the other Salmoniformes. This divergent line apparently developed mostly or entirely in the cold, fresh waters of the northern latitudes of Eurasia and North America, and gradually, over millions of years of geological upheaval and climatic change, it began sending out branches of its own. Some quickly withered and died, others survived for a time and then vanished, but others flowered and eventually sent out cautious tendrils of their own. And through this slow process of evolutionary winnowing, there eventually began to appear a glittering array of graceful, brightly colored fish that men one day would call the Salmonidae.

The common ancestor of the Salmonidae is long since extinct, but one of its earliest divergent lines led eventually to the subfamily Coregoninae, a nearly toothless group of fish whose modern living members include *Prosopium*, the Rocky Mountain whitefish; *Stenodus*, the huge, Arctic sheefish; *Coregonus*, the lake whitefish, and *Leucichthys*, the ciscoes.

A split in the line that gave rise to the whitefish led independently to evolution of another subfamily, Thymallinae, whose surviving members are the delicate and beautiful grayling of Europe and North America.

From the same common ancestor that gave rise to all the Salmonidae, another separate line developed eventually into the most complex subfamily of all, the Salmoninae, a many-splendored group of fish whose modern members include *Brachymystax*, the Siberian lenok; *Hucho*, the Huchen; *Salvelinus*, the chars; *Salmo*, the trout, and *Oncorhynchus*, the Pacific salmon.

The earliest species of *Salmo*, the trout, remains unknown and long extinct, and there is even uncertainty over which is the most primitive living species. Some believe it is the trout of Lake Ohrid, Yugoslavia, which sometimes is classified *Salmo ohridanus*. Others disagree, and consider the Lake Ohrid trout a wholly separate genus, either *Salmothymus* or *Acantholingua*. If one discounts the Lake Ohrid trout, then some of the Mediterranean-Adriatic varieties of the brown trout, *Salmo trutta*, probably rank as the most primitive surviving members of the genus *Salmo*, followed by *S. salar*, the Atlantic salmon, a trout despite its name.

A separate line from the same extinct common ancestor of *Salmo* led eventually to development of more advanced, specialized forms of trout now generally classified in the subgenus *Parasalmo*. These include the well-known trout of western North America, the cutthroat, *S. clarki*, and the rainbow, *S. gairdneri*. The same line also gave rise to the Pacific salmon, *Oncorhynchus*, which split off at some point either before or after the cutthroat and rainbow trout appeared.

Among the qualities of modern salmon and trout that man has found most endearing is their instinct to range far at sea and then return almost unerringly to their home rivers. This powerful drive reaches its peak in the steelhead and Pacific salmon, making them especially romantic and enduring symbols of stamina and strength. But migratory behavior is present to some degree in almost all salmonids and is a habit acquired very early in their evolutionary history—most likely even before the division into separate lines leading to the modern subfamilies. It happened at a time when there were waters of intermediate salinity in thousands of estuaries throughout the Northern Hemisphere, making it possible for the ancestors of trout and salmon to travel easily from the rivers to the oceans, with their vast stores of food. The ancestral fish took advantage of this rich food resource, which quickly proved to be a successful evolutionary strategy, and over time the migratory habit became deeply rooted in their instincts. Thus we see it now in their modern living relatives.

But that is about the extent of what is known or assumed of the evolutionary history of trout. Much of the theory rests on guesswork, without very much supporting evidence from the scant fossil record of ancient fish. But as one gets closer to the present, the fossil record improves, particularly in western North America, where many salmonid fossils of more recent vintage than *Eosalmo* or the Miocene Clarkia fish have been found.

Those fossils reveal glimpses of some highly unusual fish. But the strangest by far was one called *Smilodonichthys Rastrosus*, a giant "saber-toothed salmon" whose remains have been found in Oregon and California. It was named for the enormous curved breeding teeth on its upper jaw, and with these teeth and a maximum length that may have exceeded six feet, *Smilodonichthys* surely must have been a threatening specimen. Ironically, its one or two pairs of huge front teeth were virtually the only ones it had, and apparently it fed entirely on plankton.

Salmo Australis was another unusual specimen, both because it represents the southernmost occurrence of Salmonidae in North America and because it also had very odd teeth. It was found by workmen digging a cellar out of sandy soil in the village of Ajijic near the northwestern end of Lake Chapala in Mexico—at only 20 degrees north latitude, nearly 250 miles farther south than any salmonid had been found previously. *S. Australis* was a large fish, reaching nearly 40 inches in length at adulthood, with big, powerful jaws and a mouthful of formidable sharp teeth set in large round bases marked with vertical striations.

S. Australis is believed to have lived during an ice age that caused a cool, moist climate to extend southward into Mexico. Although classified within the genus *Salmo*, it was different from any other fossil or living member of the genus.

The most dominant salmonid in the recent fossil record of western North America is a trout called *Rhabdofario*, found in southern Idaho near the Oregon border. Except for a rod-like maxillary (upper jaw) bone it probably was not unlike modern trout in appearance and habit, living in lakes and perhaps growing to a maximum length of 40 inches. At first scientists believed its maxillary bone was simply too different for it to have been part of the line leading to modern cutthroat and rainbow trout, but some now say it is not unlike the maxillary which develops in modern rainbow trout as they reach old age. This has led some taxonomists to suggest that *Rhabdofario* should be abolished as a separate genus and reclassified as *Salmo*, possibly ancestral to *Parasalmo*, the modern rainbow and cutthroat trouts. Others regard the question as still open.

Dr. Robert J. Behnke of Colorado State University, one of the most eminent authorities on trout taxonomy, attempted to unravel some of the complex evolutionary relationships of western trout in an extensive monograph, "The Native Trouts of the Genus *Salmo* of Western North America," written in 1979 for the federal government. Unfortunately, it never was formally published because funds were lacking—a sad thing for scientists and anglers alike, because it is certainly the most definitive paper ever written on western trout, even though subsequent research already has altered some of its conclusions.

In it, Behnke presented a case for North America as the "center of origin" of *Parasalmo*. But he also remarked on a strange fish known as *Salmo formosanus*, "a most interesting and significant species, now perhaps extinct and known only from one river in the mountains of Formosa." Only two specimens are known to exist, both collected in 1917 "near wild country controlled by fierce headhunters."

Studies of these fish by himself and others led Behnke to conclude that *S. formosanus* is—or was—a distinct species that "may represent an early separation of the *Parasalmo* line or its direct ancestor which dispersed in Asia but became extinct except for a single river in Formosa." Unfortunately, the watershed in which *S. formosanus* was discovered was logged off many years ago and converted to agricultural use, and it seems very unlikely that any more specimens of this fish ever will be found. That is another sad thing for both anglers and scientists, for *S. formosanus* might have told us much about the recent branches of the trout's family tree.

Other than the possible *S. formosanus*, the only representative of the subgenus *Parasalmo* now living in Asia is *S. mykiss*, found in the lower Amur River of the eastern Soviet Union and along the coast of the Sea of Okhotsk to Kamchatka and the neighboring Commander Islands. But *S. mykiss* is identical to the coastal rainbow trout of North America, and Behnke suggests its foothold in Asia was gained recently, probably "no more than 11,000-12,000 years ago, or since the disappearance of the Bering Land Bridge at the end of the last glacial epoch."

Behnke's studies indicate the cutthroat "was first on the scene" in western North America and was able to colonize the waters of the upper Columbia River Basin before they were isolated by barrier falls downstream. Geographic barriers also apparently divided coastal and inland cutthroat populations, leading to divergence of the two. Glacial upheavals further split the interior group into two major subgroups, and later changes in climate and drainage patterns subdivided these into many smaller groups, each evolving and adapting to the conditions in which it found itself.

Today the range of the coastal cutthroat extends from Prince William Sound in Alaska to the Eel River in California, while the numerous interior populations are scattered all the way from southern British Columbia, Alberta, and Saskatchewan to New Mexico, Nevada, and northeast California.

The rainbow trout arose from the more primitive cutthroat, and Behnke speculates there also was a major split into coastal and inland groups early in the rainbow's history. These two populations eventually became genetically distinct, but unlike the cutthroat, the interior rainbow—which Behnke calls the "redband" trout—may again have come in contact with the coastal rainbow after the last glacial epoch, leading to some genetic mixing of the two. Another theory is offered by Dr. Gerald R. Smith of the University of Michigan, who suggests the interior "redband" trout actually may be the closest living descendant of *Rhabdofario*.

The natural range of the modern coastal rainbow extends from the Kuskokwim River of northwest Alaska to the Rio del Presidio in Mexico. The interior form inhabits the Columbia Basin east of the Cascades, except for the isolated headwaters originally colonized by the cutthroat, and is native to the desert basins of Southern Oregon, the upper Klamath Lake Basin, and the Sacramento Basin. The "redband" complex includes the famous Kamloops trout of British Columbia and the California golden trout, *S. aguabonita* and *S. gilberti*. Steelhead are found within both the coastal and interior rainbow groups, with the latter ascending the Fraser River above Hells Gate in British Columbia and the Columbia River east of the Cascade Range.

There are still other trout, native to Gulf of California drainages, at least some of which apparently are not part of either the cutthroat or rainbow line, but may have arisen separately from some early common ancestor. These include *S. chrysogaster*, the Mexican golden trout, generally considered the most primitive of the western trouts; *S. gilae*, the Gila trout of New Mexico, and *S. apache*, the Apache trout of the White Mountains of Arizona. All are distinctive in their vivid yellow or gold coloration, and *S. apache* is notable for having the largest dorsal fin of any western trout.

Dr. Robert Rush Miller, who was first to describe both *S. gilae* and *S. apache*, postulates that during the ice age the ancestral stock of *S. gilae* crossed the Baja California peninsula by way of a marine corridor near 28 degrees north latitude, or at the Isthmus of La Paz, or possibly migrated around the tip of Cape San Lucas and into the Gulf of California. From there it penetrated the Gila River drainage where it subsequently evolved in isolation to its modern form.

Miller suggested several possible origins for *S. apache*, but favors the theory that it derived from an ancestral cutthroat trout that made its way from the north into what is now the Little Colorado River basin, became isolated there and evolved into its present form.

Behnke, however, suggests all these trout are more closely related to one another than to either the rainbow or cutthroat lines, and may have evolved from "an early branching from the main line leading to cutthroat and rainbow-redband trouts."

There are still other trout, not yet formally assigned to any species, that dwell in the Rio Yaqui, Rio Casa Grandes, and Rio Mayo drainages of Mexico. Perhaps one day, when more is known about these fish, they will add to our knowledge of the evolution of western trout.

In the process of dividing and scattering themselves across the western portion of the continent, modern cutthroat and rainbow trout have split into many small but distinct local populations, and some of these have evolved in unique or unusual ways. Behnke, for example, lists 15 different subspecies of cutthroat, from the widespread coastal type to tiny isolated inland groups found only in one or two small streams.

This great diversity of forms has prompted a continuing taxonomic debate. On one side are the "lumpers," who hold that many of the differences among modern western trout populations are too small to warrant classifying them as separate subspecies. On the other side are the "splitters," who argue that populations with unique or unusual character-istics should be granted status as separate species or subspecies in order to preserve their uniqueness.

To anglers, this may seem an esoteric subject for debate, the kind of thing that could only arouse a musty scientist surrounded by mouldering books and dusty manuscripts, and to some degree it is exactly that—a long-winded technical argument. But it has implications that extend far beyond the realm of science. What it boils down to is that some people think there is special value in a name; if an animal has one all its own, it is more likely to be given respect and protection than an animal which hasn't. It is sort of like saying "birds" on the one hand and "bald eagle" on the other.

The importance of all this to sport fishermen is that the outcome of the debate could decide the future of many kinds of trout with characteris-tics that could be of great value in fisheries management.

For example, there are some populations of rainbow trout—such as the Gerrard strain of Kamloops trout in Kootenay Lake, British Columbia—that do not spawn until they are at least four or five years old, by which time they may have attained weights of 15 to 20 pounds. Such a long-lived stock could be invaluable to managers attempting to establish trophy fisheries.

Behnke writes of another example, a remarkable strain of rainbow trout he found in a tributary of the Owyhee River (coincidentally, just 12 miles from the fossil beds where *Rhabdofario* first came to light). The tributary's watershed had been devastated by grazing and the stream had been reduced to slow, intermittent pools, with a water temperature of 83 degrees, but despite these extreme conditions, the trout fed normally, came willingly to a fly and fought well. The potential management implications of a stock adapted to such temperatures, which would be lethal to most trout, can scarcely be imagined.

On the surface, there appears no reason why fish with such potentially valuable adaptations cannot be protected regardless of classification. Again, the answer is that classification—that is, the formal assignment of a name—has value in some bureaucratic quarters. Conversely, a fish without a name conferred by science may be in danger of being treated as if it were no different from any other trout.

Treating all trout as if they were alike is an approach with powerful appeal for bureaucrats, particularly on the federal level, because it promises to make their jobs much easier. After all, if a trout is just a trout, then there is no extraordinary need to protect its wild populations or the habitat which sustains them—and besides, such protection requires a lot of money and effort.

The all-alike idea also appeals to some hatchery managers; it would relieve them of the bother of separating different strains of fish in the hatchery, or of considering which ones should be planted in a particular stream or lake. The danger of this is that indiscriminate hatchery breeding soon culls out unique wild adaptations and produces homogenous populations of assembly-line fish—something which already has happened to an alarming degree. Many unique and useful adaptations, the final fruits of 100 million years of evolution, probably already have been lost in hatcheries; we cannot afford the loss of any more.

It is unfortunate that the debate between the "lumpers" and "splitters" has carried over into the bureaucratic arena. Both sides should set aside their differences long enough to join forces and insist on protection for all trout populations with unique characteristics that have value for future management, or which are valuable simply because they *are* unique—regardless of how they may be classified now or in the future.

As a practical matter, the debate over classification probably will never end. As Behnke has written, the native trouts of western North America "can never be reduced to a system of classification into species and subspecies that accurately reflects all of the degrees and nuances of evolutionary relationships." A more realistic goal, he suggests, would be to try to establish the approximate major and minor branching sequences on the basis of the evidence and "create a classification best reflecting evolutionary history."

So the arguments will go on, along with the work of trying to pinpoint the origins of trout and sorting out the many modern forms into which they have evolved. It will go on in lakes and streams, under microscopes in laboratories, and out in the countryside where the fossil bones of ancient fish lie frozen into stone.

Even if we are not able to learn everything we would like to know about the origins of trout—and very probably we shall not—at least we can learn something about the past history of these noble fish which have ascended the rivers of time to become those most favored by man.

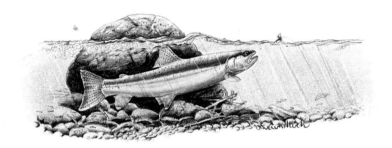

Fishing the Misty Fjords

It did not look much like a morning in May. A low overcast made the day seem dark and spurts of rain dashed hard against the wheelhouse windows on the *Phaedra Mae*. Choppy seas battered the hull until Tom Ramiskey, the boat's skipper, guided her out of the wind and into the calmer waters of Port Stewart, north of Ketchikan.

Port Stewart is where Capt. George Vancouver anchored his ships in August 1793 and sent out boats to search for the fabled Northwest Passage, which he never found. The *Phaedra Mae* was bound on a mission of a different sort—to search for cutthroat trout and steelhead in the streams flowing into Port Stewart and the countless other fjords and bays nearby. Errol Champion and I were the "explorers" and Ramiskey's boat would be our traveling home and headquarters for the week-long voyage.

We hoped for better luck than Vancouver had found.

The trip had been arranged by Dale Pihlman, president of a fledgling company called Outdoor Alaska. His idea was to set up a business to take fishermen and sightseers into the Misty Fjords wilderness northeast of Ketchikan and he had teamed up with Ramiskey, who ran the *Phaedra Mae* as a charter service out of Ketchikan.

The saltwater passages leading into the Misty Fjords are famous for their salmon fishing, but the freshwater fishing potential of the area has scarcely been explored. That was where Errol and I came in; Dale had asked us to try to find some likely spots where he and Tom could take their future customers.

It was no coincidence that our visit came at a time when the Misty Fjords were part of a raging congressional debate over which of Alaska's unspoiled lands should be preserved as wilderness. Dale, as much an environmentalist as a businessman, was hoping to prove that wilderness has economic worth as well as aesthetic value, thereby providing another good reason for Congress to preserve the Misty Fjords.

Errol and Tom and I had rendezvoused in Ketchikan and Port Stewart was our first stop. It's a narrow harbor on the eastern edge of the Cleveland Peninsula which dangles awkwardly from the Alaska mainland, and except for a few floating log rafts it probably looks much the same as it did when Vancouver chose it for an anchorage.

After the *Phaedra Mae* was safely anchored in quiet water, we launched her little Boston Whaler skiff, started the outboard and set out for the beach to explore an unnamed stream. Errol and I wore waders and fishing vests while Tom had donned a pair of boots and stuck a hefty revolver—he called it his "cannon"—into his waistband, just in case we had a surprise meeting with an angry bear.

It was a long run to the shore where a wide opening in the woods marked the location of the river, but at last we beached the boat at the edge of a tidal marsh near the river's mouth. Once ashore, we hiked upstream a little way, following the creek's meandering course through soft muskeg and back into the rainy gloom of the spruce forest. Then we began to fish our way back down, using bright flies and roll casting to avoid the brambles at our backs.

But we soon had the feeling we were searching barren water. The stream flowed evenly over a flat bed of gravel with very few sheltered spots where a fish might hold—and those few spots were empty. We had thought the stream might host a run of cutthroat and that some might still be there in early May, but if there were any they had all gone farther upstream than we had time to go. So we headed back to the *Phaedra Mae*, hoisted anchor and got under way again. Vancouver's luck was holding.

Our next stop was Spacious Bay, another anchorage a little farther north, which we reached late in the afternoon. The rain had stopped, but the day remained threatening and the wind blew dark shreds of cloud across the sky. Despite the uncertain weather, Errol and I again ran the skiff ashore, this time near the mouth of a stream called Wasta Creek. It was a noisy little stream flowing downhill over a rocky bed, filled with very dark water—almost the color of poor claret. We found nothing in its lower reaches, but a faint trail led upstream and we followed it.

About a half mile inland we came to a boggy lake that fed the creek through a pair of slow-moving outlet channels. At the far end of the lake the sun was shining brightly through a hole in the overcast, but where we stood it had begun to rain again—scattered drops that left tiny spreading rings on the surface of the twin outlet channels. But there were also much larger rings among them, the unmistakable marks of rising trout.

Errol took one channel and I waded into the other and began casting with a small Skykomish Sunrise on the end of my leader. The very first cast was met by a strong answering pull and a handsome fish came tumbling end-over-end across the surface, then began a frantic search for refuge in the brush along the channel's edge. Stopped short by the pressure of the rod, it soon came writhing to my hand—a fine cutthroat, about 15 inches long, dark silver in color with big, black leopard spots on its sides and bright crimson slashes on its lower jaw.

Twenty more fish followed in the next half hour, none larger than 16 inches but all firm and fat and brightly marked. It was preposterously easy fishing—nearly a fish on every cast—but memorable because such fishing has grown so very hard to find.

It also was very hard to leave, but the day was well spent and we still had at least an hour's run to our night anchorage. So reluctantly we reeled in and started the hike downstream, leaving fish still rising in the outlet channels.

Two sea lions popped up to inspect us and hundreds of ducks wheeled overhead as we motored back to the anchored *Phaedra Mae*. It was a wild, exciting place—Alaska as I had imagined it would be.

Tom was waiting aboard the boat with potatoes baking in the galley oven and a big bowl of tossed salad. After we had secured the skiff, raised the anchor and gotten under way, he threw steaks on the fire and we soon sat down to an enormous meal. Then, in the very last light of the long northern day, we slipped into a sheltered cove behind a point and dropped anchor in Yes Bay, a deep narrow fjord that receives the flow from Wolverine Creek, which was the reason we had come.

Next morning we motored in the skiff to the float at Yes Bay Lodge, a famous salmon-fishing resort built on the site of an abandoned cannery at the creekmouth. From the lodge a crude trail follows Wolverine Creek to its source in McDonald Lake; the creek was known to host a good run of spring steelhead.

The scale on the map showed the trail to the lake was only nine-tenths of a mile, but on foot, through muskeg and up and down granite outcrops, it seemed more like four miles. The trail was blocked frequently by deadfalls, forcing us to detour through thickets of devil's club or swamps filled with skunk-cabbage blooms and clinging black mud. In places there was no defined trail at all, only an occasional strip of survey-or's tape tied around a limb to mark the way. It was tough, hard, sweaty going, made more uncomfortable by the weather—mild and humid, with occasional spurts of rain.

Wolverine Creek is more of a full-fledged river than a creek. In its lower reaches it thunders through a narrow bedrock canyon in its eager-ness to reach the sea, but farther upstream it holds a succession of fine pools, some as large as a small lake. In the first of these we saw half a dozen large steelhead lying in the tail-out, easily visible through the clear water. The pool was too deep to wade except at the very edge, and the brushy shoreline left no room for backcasts, so we began roll casting to drop our flies where the current could carry them over the fish.

The fish were nervous in the low, clear water, and they shifted and turned as our sunken flies swung past them, but made no effort to follow. A dry fly brought the only real show of interest; a single fish followed the float and surveyed the fly closely, but still refused to take.

At length we decided to rest the pool and resumed the difficult hike upstream. After half an hour we came to a rotting lean-to on the bank of a vast pool above a split in the river, and there we were met by a breathtak-ing sight: At least 50 steelhead were scattered up and down the length of the pool. Water and the imagination of fishermen both magnify the size of fish, but even after taking both factors into account Errol and I agreed that at least a dozen of those steelhead had to exceed 20 pounds in weight.

Forgetting the weariness of the trail, we started in after them—then spent hours changing flies and lines and techniques as the fish greeted every presentation with indifference. Once again a dry fly seemed to evoke the greatest interest, and several times a fish came up closely to inspect a floating fly and follow its downstream float, sometimes even bumping it with its nose—but not one fish would actually open its mouth to take the fly.

Then Errol finally had a take on a wet pattern fished deep. The fish hit hard, but was on only a moment before the line went slack. Errol retrieved the fly to find the fish had straightened out his stout-wire hook.

My bag from the pool was a single Dolly Varden that emerged from behind a rock to intercept a sinking fly the steelhead had greeted by parting ranks to let it pass. The Dolly was a handsome two-pound fish, but it seemed a dwarf compared to the huge steelhead in the pool.

Finally we yielded to frustration and left the pool as full of fish as we had found it—even my Dolly Varden had been returned. On the downstream hike we stopped again at the first pool and found the same steelhead still lying in the tail-out, but these fish were no more willing to take than they had been before.

Then it was back to the trail, with sticky mud clinging to our boots, brambles stinging our faces and rubbery roots tripping us at each unwary step. Weary, drenched with sweat and thirsty, we finally reached the lodge—and as fate would have it, the lodge was out of beer. That prompted a dash in the skiff back to the *Phaedra Mae*, where we began depleting the ranks of cold cans in her refrigerators before we got under way for Bell Island, where we planned to spend the night.

There is another famous salmon-fishing camp at Bell Island, and when we arrived we found a skeleton crew on hand preparing for the season opening in another week. The owner invited us to use the pool, fed by hot geothermal springs, and we eagerly accepted the invitation. The steaming, buoyant water was a welcome antidote to those long hours on the trail, and we relaxed in front of the thermal jets and watched as the clouds parted to reveal a gathering host of stars. When we finally trooped back to the *Phaedra Mae* at dockside, the sky was alight with the silent shifting curtains of the northern lights.

Next morning we left Bell Island and entered the heart of the Misty Fjords wilderness, a land where deep wounds left by mighty glaciers have been flooded by the sea. The evidence of this violent geological past is preserved in shadowed, somber fjords surrounded by great folds of granite—one of the most spectacular and beautiful landscapes on earth.

As we turned southeast into Behm Canal, a long line of snowy peaks unfolded before us, row upon row of whitecapped ridges extending as far as the eye could see. From our vantage point they appeared impenetrable, but the map showed these walls of rock were pierced by fjords whose entrances were invisible until the traveler was almost upon them. We passed several such entrances, narrow chasms opening suddenly to reveal long veins of water thrusting back into the mountain fastnesses, then disappearing quickly behind us—almost as if a secret door had been briefly opened, then quickly closed.

Then we came to the fjord that was our destination and turned into it, entering a narrow passage with great walls of gray rock rising 3,000 feet on either side. Here and there the walls were stained with silver waterfalls plunging down from snow on the clifftops, or hanging in frozen drifts in shadowed fissures in the rock. A few wind-twisted spruce had gained a fragile purchase on the walls, and these stood out like solitary climbers halfway up the rock, with great wispy chains of moss hanging from their limbs.

The sea in the narrow passageway ahead was as smooth as a ribbon of glass, and it seemed a long way up to the sky. The chart showed nearly 1,800 feet of water beneath our keel, so there was nearly a mile of distance from clifftop to seafloor.

We cruised for several miles through this awesome scenery until suddenly one wall of the fjord opened to disclose a bay at the foot of a narrow valley with great peaks and snowfields looming on every side. Out of the valley flowed a river, entering the bay between grass-covered headlands in a perfect, park-like setting. We dropped anchor in the bay and Errol and I climbed into the skiff for the run to the mouth of the river.

Reaching shore, we pulled the skiff up into the deep grass near the river's mouth and began the hike upstream. A little way up the valley opened into a great natural amphitheater, with tiered rows of stone rising to the snowline on either side and waterfalls streaking down to the valley floor. The river whispered softly as it carried the snow-cold water in graceful curves toward the sea, and the water was as clear as the mountain air so that every detail of the fine golden gravel on the river bottom was exposed in sharp relief.

The river ran alternately in smooth, deep glides and burst into noisy, rock-strewn rapids, sparkling in the shafts of sunlight that poured down from beyond the peaks. There were tracks of deer and bear on the sandbars, and high on the slopes we could see a group of mountain goats cavorting near the snowline. It was a scene too perfect for pictures or for words; of all the other rivers I have ever seen or heard about, there is none that could compare.

But where were the fish? The river was so clear that if it held trout of any kind we surely should have seen them. Bleached bones from last autumn's salmon run lay half-buried in the sand, but there was no sign of any living fish.

And then at last we found them: In the pool above the first rapid, well back, lying in deep water behind a lichen-stained rock, were five steelhead, clean and bright and fresh from the sea. It had to be; the river was too perfect in every other way not to host such a noble race of fish.

We tried for them cautiously with small flies fished just under the surface on fine leaders, and then with dry flies and a riffle hitch, but the fish were spooky and nervous in the clear water and moved away as the flies passed overhead. At first I was frustrated, but after a while I found myself past caring; it was exhilarating just to be there, where so few other men had ever been, and to see these magnificent sights that so few other men had ever seen. The river suddenly seemed a hallowed place, a place where the steelhead were better left undisturbed, where it seemed wrong even to leave a footprint in the sand along its shores.

I quit fishing then and concentrated on trying to remember every detail of this enchanted place, knowing that very likely I would never have another chance to see it. And when it finally was time for us to leave, I left sadly, though I knew my memories would be greater reward than any trophy fish could be.

In the days to come we explored other rivers and saw more magnificent country. We watched eagles spiral overhead and traveled with a school of porpoises that rode the bow wave of the *Phaedra Mae* so closely we could nearly reach out and touch them. We hiked along streambanks where the only human footprints were our own, and cruised along great empty waterways where no ships ever came in sight. We were alone, just we three, in a country still untouched by man, and it felt very good to be there. I am not sure I have felt as good anywhere else.

Looking back on it now, I suppose in one sense our trip was a failure because we had largely failed to find the object of our search. Going in, we had known little about the timing of the runs in the rivers of the Misty Fjords, and we found fish in only a few of them. Even when we found them, we were not always able to catch them. But we saw enough to know that the wilderness has a wealth of good water, and surely its rivers and lakes must hold cutthroat and steelhead in abundance at times. I envy those who will carry on the exploration and finally establish the timing of those runs.

But even if there were no runs, the scenery is so spectacular that everything else is secondary. If there is one place in the world where an angler can go fishless and not be unhappy about it, it is in the Misty Fjords.

Both the fishing and the scenery still are there. The congressional battle finally was resolved and most of the Misty Fjords have been formally classified as wilderness, off-limits to any permanent habitation or alteration by man.

The wilderness area includes a certain unnamed river that flows through an enchanted valley and whispers softly as it carries snow-cold water in graceful curves toward the sea. In the spring it welcomes home bright steelhead that hold nervously in its deepest pools, and in the fall the salmon return to it and leave their bones to bleach in its golden sand.

It is a river I may never see again, but it will always flow through my memory, through my dreams—perhaps even through my soul.

A Well-Traveled Fish

The story of the diplomat and the salmon is one of the most charming chapters in Northwest angling lore. T.W. Lambert was among the first to tell it in his book, *Fishing in British Columbia*. His version, published in 1907, goes like this:

"There is another story very popular in the West, relating what happened at the time when the great fur companies held the country and were disputing and even fighting for its possession. The (British) Imperial Government sent out some illustrious diplomat to report on the situation, and he described the country as of no value and so hopeless that 'even the salmon would not take the fly.' It is a tradition in British Columbia that on this ground the now flourishing states of Idaho, Montana, Washington and Oregon were handed over to the Americans."

It would be ironic if there were any truth to the story, for we now know that Pacific salmon will take flies, at least under some circumstances. But it's easy to understand how the diplomat—if there ever really was such a person—could easily have grown disgusted at the dour behavior of the Pacific fish when he was used to the magnificent Atlantic salmon of the British Isles. In fact, such an attitude would have been typical of most men, who never seem quite satisfied with the hand that nature deals them.

That was certainly true of the men who settled the Northwest; even though their adopted country was favored by great natural runs of salmon, steelhead, cutthroat and char, the settlers weren't content: They wanted Atlantic salmon, too. So did the men who settled many another far-flung land, and so they do today; wherever there are rivers and men to fish them, those men will wish for Atlantic salmon.

There is hardly any mystery in this. The Atlantic salmon reaches a greater size than any other trout (as a member of the genus *Salmo*, it is a trout despite its common name). It also has a character and reputation all its own, a mystique that has caused many anglers to regard it as the ultimate fly-rod challenge in fresh water.

The Atlantic salmon also is by far the most prestigious of all fish, a consequence of many years of private ownership of the best salmon rivers. Only the very wealthy can afford access to these rivers, and this has made salmon fishing an aristocratic sport, with the best reserved for kings and dukes and famous statesmen (or diplomats). That's another reason why men of all nations want salmon in their rivers; they envy the status of those who fish for salmon, and the opportunity to catch one is a way for even the most humble commoner to feel—if only for a moment—that he is on equal footing with a king.

All this has made the Atlantic salmon the world's most well-traveled, oft-transplanted fish. But the salmon also is a most particular fish, both in its habits and its choice of habitat, and only recently has man learned very much about either one of these. His earlier lack of knowledge led to the failure of many attempts to introduce salmon to foreign waters, and when he succeeded it was largely a matter of luck.

The eager settlers of New Zealand were among the first to attempt long-distance transplants of Atlantic salmon; they also have been among the most persistent. They began way back in 1868 when the provincial government of Otago on the South Island received some salmon eggs from the Tay and Severn rivers in Britain. These were hatched and reared to an average length of about six inches and 500 were released in the Waiwera River—the beginning of what turned out to be 40 years of effort to establish salmon in New Zealand waters.

During those four decades, eggs were imported from many sources and salmon were planted in many waters on both the North and South Islands. Many fish were released into river systems that drained to salt water in hopes the salmon would migrate to sea and return as large adults, just like their European ancestors. But despite all the hope and effort, to this day there never has been a single authenticated report of a seagoing Atlantic salmon returning to any New Zealand river (although transplanted Pacific salmon have done so for many years). In fact, most of the Atlantic salmon planted in New Zealand waters seem simply to have vanished.

But not all of them. A 1908 shipment of eggs from Canada hatched into fry that were liberated in a tributary of the Upukerora River, which flows into Lake Te Anau, a huge natural lake near Fjordland National Park in the southwest corner of the South Island. The next year another shipment was obtained from the British Isles, and fry from these eggs also were placed in the Upukerora. Eggs from other stocks, including the English Test, the Dee, the Wye, and even the German Rhine, were hatched and released at various times into the same stream or into Lake Te Anau itself. It is impossible now to say which of these plants succeeded, but at least one of them did. However, contrary to the hopes of their liberators, the fish did not migrate out of the lake to the sea; instead, they stayed where they were, feeding on the rich aquatic life in Lake Te Anau and running up its tributaries to spawn.

Rich as it was, Lake Te Anau could not provide growth comparable to the sea. G. Stokell, in his book *Fresh Water Fishes of New Zealand*, says the average weight of 114 salmon taken from Lake Te Anau in 1932 was 4.2 pounds—a nice-sized fish, to be sure, but no larger than a precocious sea-run grilse. Stokell also mentioned a mounted specimen of 29½ inches which he found hanging on the wall at the Te Anau Hotel, a fish which might have weighed as much as nine pounds. While that was certainly exceptional for Lake Te Anau, it would be a small fish by the standards of most seagoing salmon.

Today, rainbow and brown trout greatly outnumber salmon in Lake Te Anau, but in Lakes Gunn and Fergus—part of the watershed of the Eglinton River which flows into Lake Te Anau—Atlantic salmon are still abundant. Salmon up to eight pounds have been reported from Lake Gunn, although I saw none of that size during a visit to the lake in 1980.

Atlantic salmon also are taken occasionally from Lake Manopouri, downstream from Lake Te Anau, and sometimes from the Waiau River between those lakes, and they may exist in a few other New Zealand waters. That seems little to show for the decades of work New Zealanders have invested in these temperamental fish, but it is perhaps a measure of the difficulty of transplanting Atlantic salmon that New Zealand's experience ranks as one of the more successful.

One of the earliest attempts to transplant Atlantic salmon in North America was in the Delaware River, where the New Jersey state Fish Commission planted salmon fry for several years in the early 1870s. Some of these fish apparently survived, went to sea and returned, for in 1877 a few salmon weighing as much as nine pounds were taken from the Delaware and a fish of 24 pounds was reported the following year. But despite this promising start, no effort was made to nurture the fledgling run and it soon disappeared.

Atlantic salmon also were planted in Yellowstone Lake shortly before the turn of the century, but these fish also failed to become established, possibly because they were unable to compete with the large population of native cutthroat.

Perhaps mindful of the legendary diplomat's harsh judgment of their land, British Columbia fisheries authorities tried during the early years of this century to establish runs of Atlantic salmon in some of their waters. "Atlantic salmon have been introduced into the waters about Vancouver Island, and quite a number of specimens have been reported as having been taken in some years by anglers," the pioneer biologist J.R. Dymond reported. However, Dymond was able to collect only two specimens for his own studies, and both were small: "One had been taken in Cowichan Lake, September 3, 1913; it was less than six inches long. The other, eleven inches in length and nine ounces in weight, was taken in the Lower Cowichan River on May 31, 1926."

Noting the diminutive size of these fish, Dymond went on to report that "in the opinion of A.A. Easton, fisheries inspector at Duncan (Vancouver Island), the Atlantic salmon introduced into that district may have stayed in the lakes and rivers, as they have done in New Zealand, where they act like landlocked fish." Dymond concluded his report by writing: "The planting of this species in British Columbia waters has now been discontinued, on account of the lack of success attending its introduction."

So another experiment ended in failure. But it would have taken much more than a dubious record of earlier results to deter the indefatigable Edward Ringwood Hewitt, the famous angler, innovator, and author. Hewitt began experimenting with Atlantic salmon in his private water on

New York's little Neversink shortly after World War I. Over the years, he imported salmon eggs from Norway and Scotland, hatched them and planted the fry in his beloved Neversink. Yet despite his determination and enterprise, his efforts also went for naught; although two anglers later reported catching and releasing Atlantic salmon in the Neversink, there is no documented record of any of these fish ever having been seen again.

One of the few successful experiments in transplanting Atlantic salmon, and surely the most widely publicized, was that carried out by the state of Oregon in Hosmer Lake. The lake itself covers an old creek channel meandering across an alpine meadow that once was a pumice plain, ringed by spectacular snowcapped volcanic cones and a labyrinth of twisted lava flows surrounded by thick forests of lodgepole pine. Fed by Quinn Creek, which flows at a nearly constant temperature of 42 degrees, Hosmer measures only 11 feet at its deepest point and most of it is much shallower. It is an exceptionally rich lake, with enormous spring hatches of mayflies, caddisflies and damselflies, and few better trout environments could be imagined.

Until 1957 the lake was occupied only by a few brook trout and large numbers of carp and roach which had been introduced sometime before 1940. It was known then as Mud Lake, probably because the carp kept the pumice bottom stirred up constantly so that the water was never clear. The lake was chemically treated in the fall of 1957 and the carp and roach were removed, although some brook trout survived—probably by taking refuge in Quinn Creek.

In 1951, the state of Oregon obtained 10,000 eggs from Gaspe Bay sea-run Atlantic salmon stock, provided by the Quebec Department of Game and Fisheries. The eggs were hatched at the Wizard Falls Hatchery on the Metolius River, but the fry proved extremely hard to handle; at first they would not feed, and many lingered on the bottom of the hatchery raceway and eventually died of bacterial gill disease. About 90 percent of the first lot died in the fry stage, but there were still enough fish left alive after five years to breed a second generation, which proved somewhat more adaptable to the hatchery environment.

A second shipment of Gaspe Bay eggs arrived at Wizard Falls in 1958, adding to the stock already on hand. In the spring of that same year, the first liberations of Atlantic salmon from the original lot were made into Hosmer Lake—6,015 yearling fish averaging six inches and 9,014 fry averaging three inches. The lake remained closed to fishing until 1961 when it was opened under regulations that allowed anglers to keep a single salmon. State officials estimated that 2,956 salmon were caught that first year, the largest measuring 27½ inches and weighing 6¼ pounds. The average of all fish caught was 20 inches.

Removal of the carp had allowed the suspended particles of silt to settle out of the water and the combination of the clear, shallow water and pumice bottom made it possible for anglers to see fish cruising at great distance. The salmon also proved enthusiastic risers to the heavy hatches of mayflies and caddisflies, and these factors soon made Hosmer a favorite spot for dry-fly fishermen. The lake's spectacular alpine beauty and exotic fishing also made the name "Mud" seem singularly inappropriate, so in 1962 it was officially changed to Hosmer Lake, in honor of Paul Hosmer, a naturalist of local renown.

That same year the fishing regulations were changed to catch-and-release and fly-fishing-only with barbless hooks, and they have remained so ever since.

Oregon fisheries authorities had great hopes that the Hosmer Lake salmon would reproduce by spawning in Quinn Creek. The fish did indeed spawn, but winter anchor ice destroyed their eggs. That made it necessary for the state to take on the costly business of maintaining a large hatchery stock of salmon in order to replant the lake periodically. The investment paid off, however, for Hosmer's reputation quickly spread far beyond the borders of Oregon, with unexpected benefits for the state. A 1971 study estimated that 90 percent of the anglers visiting the lake had come from out of state—a rich source of income for the Oregon license fund and a significant source of business for the local economy.

From 1962 to 1970, Hosmer Lake provided wonderful fishing. Most of the fish measured 20 inches or more, with quite a few in the four- to five-pound class and some larger. Although this was still only grilse-sized by sea-run standards, the opportunity to fish for salmon provided a marvelous new experience for Western anglers.

But the fishery began a slow decline in the early 1970s. One problem was that the salmon had a bad habit of escaping from the lake. Harkening back to their sea-run ancestry, many yearling fish tried to migrate by swimming out over the top of a crude outlet dam during periods of high water. Water spilling over the dam flows about 100 yards and disappears into a sump in the porous lava; fish washed down this sump are never seen again, and many were lost this way.

The disappearance of yearling fish was accompanied by a natural die-off of older fish in the lake, and together these factors established a downward trend that reached a low point in September 1975, when all 4,317 yearling salmon remaining at the Wizard Falls Hatchery were stocked in an effort to restore the Hosmer Lake fishery.

In the years since, the fishing has been up and down, but mostly down, defying the best efforts of biologists to restore it to its early days of glory. In 1982 it hit bottom; in the spring of that year, biologists estimated the total population of salmon in the lake was only 75 fish. A fall plant brought the population up to several thousand fish by the following spring, but by summer's end most of them were gone.

Fish escapement during high water has remained a serious problem, but not the only one: The shallow, clear water of Hosmer Lake makes the salmon especially vulnerable to attack from a burgeoning population of ospreys and it is not uncommon for these magnificent birds to take at least 50 fish a day. A thriving group of otters also takes its share. Another problem is growing evidence of genetic stagnation among the breeding stock, which has not had an infusion of new blood since the last shipment of eggs in 1958. The offspring of these fish have shown an increasing lack of vigor and an ever-higher incidence of albinoism and other symptoms of inbreeding within a small, closed population.

In the fall of 1983, two significant steps were taken to try to solve some of these problems: Local fly fishermen joined state workers to repair the outlet dam and make it more difficult for fish to escape from the lake, and 20,000 landlocked salmon eggs from Maine were received at the Wizard Falls Hatchery. The Maine fish, from the so-called "Grand Lake Stream" stock of landlocked salmon, presumably lack the smolting instinct that has caused so many of the Gaspe Bay fish to leave the lake; they also should add fresh vigor to the hatchery stock. But it will take several years for the Maine fish to prove themselves, and at this point the future of the Hosmer Lake salmon fishery is highly uncertain.

The early success of Atlantic salmon in Hosmer Lake is all the more remarkable when one considers that efforts to introduce these fish into nearby waters ended in total failure. Fish from the Gaspe Bay stock also were planted in several other lakes in the Oregon Cascades, including Sparks and Davis, two well-known fly-fishing waters, but only a few survived long enough to be caught by anglers. The rest died out.

The good early fishing at Hosmer also inspired Washington state anglers to lobby for an Atlantic salmon experiment within their own state, and the Washington Game Department finally acquiesced and obtained some of Oregon's Wizard Falls stock. The fish were held in a hatchery while a search was made for a suitable lake to put them in. That proved to be a difficult task, for even though the state had more than 8,000 lakes to choose from, not a single one could be found with characteristics as favorable as those of Hosmer Lake.

Chopaka Lake, a popular, scenic, fly-fishing-only lake in the Okanogan country of north central Washington, finally was chosen as the best candidate, even though it had only a few similarities to Hosmer. In the spring of 1973, Chopaka received a plant of 7,920 Atlantic salmon averaging 10 inches.

Ken Williams, the state biologist assigned to monitor the experiment, later reported that the Atlantic salmon began to loose weight as soon as they were planted in the lake, and by fall they had become "emaciated . . . with significant numbers on the verge of starvation." Williams also put his finger on the reason why: For years the Washington Game Department had planted enormous numbers of rainbow trout in Chopaka Lake; more than 50,000 had gone into the lake in 1972 alone. In retrospect, it was hardly surprising that a small number of Atlantic salmon were unable to compete with a large, well-established population of rainbow trout.

"The salmon appeared to have a difficult time adjusting," Williams reported. "Salmon would meander slowly but constantly back and forth over a large but definable area. If they got too close to the trout, they were immediately subjected to strong acts of aggression, including nipping. In every case observed, salmon were submissive to trout aggression. Aggression was never noted among the salmon."

The Chopaka experiment ended in failure, but the next year the state tried again in another lake—this one with an environment about as different from the natural habitat of sea-run Atlantic salmon as it would be possible to find. It was called Quail Lake, actually little more than a pond formed by irrigation seepage in the hot desert near the little town of Othello in central Washington. Surrounded by barren basalt outcrops and clumps of sage and bitterbrush and swept by howling winds and sandstorms, the scenery around Quail Lake probably bears a closer resemblance to the surface of Mars than it does a salmon river.

But Quail Lake had produced large trout in the past, and its trout population was small enough that biologists felt it would not pose a competitive threat to the salmon. So, in October, 1974, 580 Atlantic salmon averaging 10 to 12 inches were planted in the lake.

When the lake was sampled eight months later, the fish averaged 18½ inches—a nearly unheard-of rate of growth approaching an inch a month in some cases. It looked as if Washington state finally had found a lake where Atlantic salmon could survive and thrive.

But the jubilation over Quail Lake was short-lived. The salmon were so efficient in feeding on the lake's aquatic insect population that they soon destroyed it, leaving themselves with nothing to eat. A second plant of yearling fish in 1975 scarcely grew at all, and the older fish—those which had grown so rapidly during their first year in the lake—grew thin and sluggish and began to die. Quail Lake turned out to be a flash in the pan; no more salmon were planted there.

However, some Atlantic salmon were planted in a third lake, a small, high-altitude tarn in the mountains of the Olympic Peninsula. At first they did well, feeding on a natural population of scuds, and anglers who hiked into the lake two years after it was stocked caught salmon weighing more than three pounds. But the state has since ended its Atlantic salmon program, mainly for lack of success, so there will be no further stocking of this lake.

There is more than a little irony in the fact that Washington state finally gave up trying to establish Atlantic salmon in its own waters, because it is playing a vital role in the effort to restore salmon to the New England rivers where they were once native. Several different stocks of Atlantic salmon, including some descendants of the original Gaspe Bay-Hosmer Lake fish, are being held in saltwater pens in Puget Sound to provide eggs and fry for planting in New England streams. Puget Sound was chosen as the holding site because, unlike most New England harbors, it remains free of ice in winter.

In a way it is sad to visit the floating pens and see these great fish in such small enclosures, with walls of mesh that keep them from fulfilling their age-old instinct to head for the open sea. But there is consolation in knowing they may hold the seeds of restoration for the faraway rivers of New England, whose original salmon stocks were wiped out by dams and pollution a century ago.

It also seems entirely in keeping with the salmon's reputation as a well-traveled fish that some are being held in Pacific waters for the benefit of restoring vanished runs in the Atlantic. And surely that is not the end of the story; ambitious Atlantic salmon stocking programs are now under way in the Great Lakes and in other waters, and more will certainly follow. As man continues to learn about the salmon, it also is reasonable to expect that more transplants will be successful than in the past.

So the salmon's travels are bound to continue, and perhaps one day fisheries biologists will even find a way to make it more than just a token resident of the Pacific Northwest. Though that might cause some temporary restlessness in the immortal sleep of a certain legendary British diplomat, I think anglers would welcome it.

I know I would.

Price's Lake

It had been a long time since my last visit to Price's Lake. Each year I'd plan to go there, just as I had gone so often in the past, but something always seemed to interfere. I'd postpone the trip, thinking that I'd get another chance, but somehow those second chances never came. Before I knew it, five years had passed.

Finally I set a date to return and vowed this time I'd let nothing interfere. At last the day came and Randy and I set out on a fresh spring morning over roads still wet with rain.

I went with some misgivings, remembering that often I'd returned to a favorite water after a long absence and found many changes, seldom any for the better. Price's Lake was well off the beaten track, but not so far that it was invulnerable to change.

I wondered if it would still be anything like it was on the very first day I fished it, nearly 20 years before. I caught nothing that day, but I watched another fisherman take a four-pound rainbow on a fast-stripped Muddler Minnow back in the weeds. It was a fine bright trout, one that would have been a trophy from any lake, and I remember wishing keenly that it had been my fish instead of his. Just the sight of it—plus the knowledge that here was a lake capable of producing such fish—inspired me to return. And for the next few years I did so often.

It never was an easy place to reach. The dirt road was always rutted and always wet and ended a quarter of a mile from the lake. Near its end was a ramshackle cabin surrounded by second-growth firs and rusting hulks of cars, machinery, and other detritus from someone's lifetime in the woods. An old couple lived there and rented boats on the lake and sometimes when I stopped to pay they would invite me into their cluttered kitchen for a mug of steaming coffee.

The kitchen was a period piece, with pots and pans hanging from nails driven in the walls and a linoleum floor that had been buckled by the damp until it undulated like the surface of the lake when the wind was up. While I sipped coffee the old man would always say the fishing had been good and if I tried a Yellow Professor I would surely catch my share. He would say that even if the fishing had been poor.

The road beyond the cabin was little more than a muddy trail. It led down through an old apple orchard that was under attack from the woods, which had sent fir seedlings as scouts to grow among the apple trees. It was a battle the orchard was bound to lose, but each fall its defiant trees still bent under a heavy weight of fruit, and every spring their blossoms lit the trail.

The road finally petered out at the edge of a swamp and from there it was a 10-minute walk over a boardwalk to the lake. The boardwalk, fashioned of split cedar sections laid across a pair of wooden rails, followed a zig-zag course through dense thickets of fern and skunk cabbage and scattered pools of dark water with great old cedars growing out of them. The cedars trailed long strands of moss and snake-like vines and their thick foliage held the rain and dripped it slowly. It was a dark and eerie place, filled with the moist scent of slowly rotting leaves and wood.

Often enough the odor of rotting wood came from the boardwalk. Although sections of it had been replaced from time to time, decay had begun the very moment the new planks were set in place and some always were broken or missing at vital points along the way. The gaps revealed stagnant pools of black water and sticky ooze below, and the only way to get across was to walk tight-rope fashion on the narrow wooden rails. It was not an easy thing to do, especially if one was carrying a heavy pack, or if mosquitoes decided to attack—as they often did just at the instant when one's balance seemed in greatest peril.

Even on a dark day, stepping out of the shadowy swamp and into the open would leave a fisherman blinded and blinking while his eyes adjusted to the sudden light. When he could see again, he would find himself looking out on a leaning dock attached to unsteady posts driven into the muddy bottom of the lake. An assortment of battered wooden rowboats was kept tied to the dock, and these were the source of the old couple's income. It was a monopoly business; no one in his right mind would have tried to carry a boat over the boardwalk, and float tubes had yet to come in fashion.

But the rowboats always lacked something—sometimes something vital, like an intact hull, but more often something a little less essential, like an oarlock, a seat or a matched pair of oars. Ingenuity usually could provide at least a temporary substitute for whatever was missing, but when the substitutes had been devised and a boat was as seaworthy as a fisherman could make it . . . well, usually that was just the beginning of his problems.

Price's Lake is one of the wettest places in a state famous for its rain. Annual rainfall at the lake exceeds 100 inches, and rarely a day goes by without at least a little rain; more often there's a lot. I've spent days there when I had the feeling that the rain and the lake were in a race to see which could be first to sink my boat—the lake seeping or spurting in through cracks in an old, poorly caulked hull, while the rain hemorrhaged from clouds that had gathered an oceanful of it in their long journey across the Pacific. Sometimes I'd bail until I could barely lift my arms, but then I'd drift over the watery grave of a sunken rowboat, dimly visible on the bottom. There were many sunken boats on the bottom of Price's Lake, and the sight of one always was an inspiration to keep on bailing.

The reward for all this risk and effort was a chance to catch large rainbow, Eastern brook, or cutthroat trout, and Price's Lake is the only place I've ever fished where it was possible to catch all three. It also was a lake ideally suited to the fly, shallow and weedy and filled with massive stumps and snags. On spring days it produced good hatches of large mayflies, and at dusk blizzards of smaller mayflies and caddisflies would rise from its surface. Later it would come alive with squirming damselfly nymphs searching for stumps or stems to crawl out upon and hatch. Sporadic hatches continued even in the fall, and sometimes late in October there would be a great flight of termites from the woods and the awkward insects would fall on the water and set off a frenzied rise of fish.

It also was a lake with a firmly established place in local angling lore. It had given up many large fish—brook trout to five pounds and rainbow to seven, if you could believe the tales—and any lake which produces trout or trout stories of that size is bound to attract a large following of anglers. Among the Price's Lake "regulars" were some of the Northwest's most famous fishermen, including Enos Bradner, outdoor editor of *The Seattle Times* and one of the founders of the Washington Fly Fishing Club. Bradner caught two brook trout in Price's Lake which still are the largest ever entered in the records of the club, and it was on Price's Lake where Bradner and Frank Headrick perfected a fly pattern they dubbed the "Dandy Green Nymph" which has since become a Northwest standard.

Price's Lake also has an unusual natural history. Geologists say it was created by an enormous earthquake that pushed up a scarp to block a stream flowing through a gentle valley. Water backed up behind the scarp, forming the lake and flooding a stand of huge firs and cedars; the trees died and gradually rotted away at the waterline, but their stumps were preserved under water. Based on the age of the stumps, geologists believe the earthquake occurred between 1,100 and 1,300 years ago.

I'd heard the stories about Price's Lake and went there to see if they were true. That first visit 20 years ago convinced me that they were, and after that I fished it many times—in spring and fall, in the usual rain or during rare spells of sunshine, on calm mornings or windy afternoons. I found it an intriguing and strangely enigmatic water, slow to share its secrets. Often it was sullen and unyielding, devoid of any apparent sign of life, and occasionally it was grudgingly friendly and granted me a fish now and then. But every once in a very great while it could be unbelievably generous, both in numbers and size of trout.

Once I went there with Bradner. He was an old man by then but age had not impaired his skill. By the day's end I had caught more fish, but the ones he caught were much larger. Another time I went with Ward McClure and we found the way blocked by a fir tree that had fallen across the road. Somehow we had forgotten to bring along an ax and a dull machete was the only cutting tool we had. It took nearly an hour to cut through the tree and there were blisters on our hands when we finished, but we went on to the lake anyway. We found it in a stingy mood and fished painfully through an afternoon of blinding rain with only three small trout to show for our efforts.

Ed Foss and Vince Sellen joined me there one day when the wind blew so hard we swore there were whitecaps in our coffee cups, but we caught fish anyway. And once when I went alone the old couple in the cabin said I was the first person they had seen in more than a week. Nevertheless, the old man still said the fishing had been good and if I used a Yellow Professor I would surely catch my share.

There were days when I did catch my share. Once I caught a brook trout of nearly 2½ pounds, the largest I have taken. I landed many rainbow over two pounds and some over three, mostly on dry flies during mayfly hatches in the spring, and one day after taking several brook trout and rainbows, I caught the first cutthroat I had ever taken there—the first time I had ever caught all three species in a day.

I learned to know the lake in all its moods. I grew to love it in the spring, when the apple blossoms burst open in the old orchard, the skunk cabbage flashed its yellow blooms like lanterns in the darkness of the swamp and everywhere around the lake the cottonwoods and alders and maples were in fresh green leaf. But I loved it just as much in the fall when those once-fresh leaves would change to rusty red and gold and the slightest breeze would shake them loose and send them gliding in gentle spirals down to the water. I even loved it on days when the woods dripped rain and the sky was heavy with the dark promise of more, or when a chilling fog settled down on the water and blotted out the hills so that it seemed as if I had floated off the earth into a mysterious gray void.

More often than not I fished with only ducks or muskrats or a solitary heron for company, and sometimes at dusk I'd hear the quavering howl of a coyote close at hand or the sound of something large crashing through the nearby brush. All these things were a part of the peculiar charm of Price's Lake; it had taken hold of me, and I found it a strangely wild and beautiful place.

But some things did change in the years that I fished it. The old couple's cabin, which stood on land leased from a logging company, was swept by fire one winter and the old man suffered burns. They took him away to a rest home and when he was unable to return the logging company canceled the lease and closed the road. A new road was opened to the opposite side of the lake with a trail down a steep hillside to the shore.

About the same time, responding to lobbying by fly fishing clubs, the state declared Price's Lake a "wild trout" water. No more trout would be stocked, and those already in the lake would be allowed to spawn naturally in its two small inlet streams. Fishermen would have to use artificial flies or lures and release all the trout they caught.

I fished it a few times after that, using the new road and the new trail and carrying in my own boat. The lake itself had seemed the same and I enjoyed it just as much as always.

But five years had passed since my last visit there. And now, as I drove up the eastern flank of the Olympic Peninsula, I could see that ugly real-estate "developments" had metastasized far up into the foothills. The sight of them kept me in suspense until we drew closer to our destination and I saw with relief that the spreading blight had yet to reach into the secluded valley of Price's Lake.

The dirt road leading to the lake was just the same as it had been the last time I had driven it and I found the trailhead easily, though the trail itself showed little evidence of use. It also seemed a little longer and steeper than I'd remembered it, but then all trails are beginning to seem that way to me.

Randy helped me with the boat and we got it down to the lake and set up our rods and pushed away from shore. There was no one else in sight, but it would be wrong to say we had the lake entirely to ourselves; three ospreys circled overhead and two of them were busy building up a nest—a knobby-looking affair in the top of an old fir near the shoreline of the lake. We watched them carry limbs and branches to add to the considerable bundle they already had assembled.

The day was mixed with changing patterns of sun and cloud and drizzle and a variable breeze. The water was cold and clear and the weeds were barely beginning to sprout from the bottom, though the annual crop of water lilies already was appearing near the shore. During periods when the sun was out and the lake was flat, big dark *Callibaetis* mayfly duns popped to the surface and hoisted their wings like tiny sails. Occasionally a trout would follow one up and take it, but most of the fish were feeding on the nymphs, leaving only little wrinkles on the surface to show what they were doing. We put up a size 12 *Callibaetis* nymph on a floating line and quickly found action.

The first fish was a rainbow, strong and fat and firm. The second was a cutthroat, dressed in a beautiful shade of olive with bright red slashes under its lower jaw. The third was a brook trout, also handsomely marked with bright pink and lemon-yellow spots floating in the sunset colors on its sides. All were wild, naturally spawned trout, their fins perfectly shaped, their colors those nature gave them. It would be hard to find three prettier trout anywhere. Once before I had caught all three species in a single day on Price's Lake, but this was the first time I'd ever done it back-to-back.

All the fish were fat and in good condition, but each was only about 11 inches long and I remembered that Price's Lake was capable of better. The next fish proved the point; it was a bright rainbow that jumped high and took out line and weighed a little over two pounds when I finally brought it in. It was followed by another rainbow only a little smaller, then by two smaller brook trout.

We fished leisurely with time out for lunch and a couple of newt-hunting expeditions. Price's Lake abounds with rough-skinned newts and they seem to have a special fascination for kids. Randy caught a couple and kept them as temporary "pets" until we were through fishing; then, like the trout, they were returned to the lake.

At last we steered the boat back through the ancient stumps to the muddy launch at the foot of the trail, then loaded our gear and started up the hill. Behind us the lake sparkled in the afternoon sun, still the same lonely, wild and beautiful place that it had always been. And I was glad.

Some places are perfect just the way they are. Price's Lake is one of them.

Summer

I f you go out on a summer morning when the day is just breaking you will find the river in its loveliest mood. The air is cool and fresh and full of promise and the river seems hushed and quiet as it flows through meadows still sparkling wet with morning dew. Deer slip down from the woods to drink in the cool eddies, and you may see a great blue heron standing stock-still in the shallows; it has begun its fishing day even before you have begun yours.

Winter's violence and river-changing floods are a fading memory now, for by summer the river has assumed the shape it will hold for the remainder of the year. With the slow passage of the long warm summer days it will shrink ever deeper in its channel until by August it will begin to show its bones—the bleached white water-blasted rocks that shaped its currents during the high water of seasons past. If you look at them closely you may see the vacant shucks of stonefly nymphs that crawled up on them to hatch and enjoy a brief caper in the air during the latter days of May or early June. Perhaps you also will see some tiny empty tubes of gravel, calling cards left by caddis pupae that have long since passed through their miraculous metamorphosis into flies.

Yet even during August's low water the river still bustles with life. Steelhead and cutthroat fry that hatched in April are busy feeding in the shallows and the long pale ghosts of Dolly Varden stalk them there. Spring Chinook salmon have returned to the river for their long rest before spawning and they hold in the deeper quiet pools, rolling noisily in the twilight and sending ripples all the way to the shore. And even when the current subsides to its weakest flow the summer steelhead somehow are still able to find where it mingles with the sea and follow it upstream.

During the hot, still, lazy days of August the steelhead pause to rest in shaded runs and there they may be tempted by a floating fly or a gleaming bit of fur and feathers offered at the end of a long floating line. Then, if an angler is lucky, he may witness the heart-stopping sight of a fresh-run summer fish rising to a high-floating fly, or the great swirl of a strong subsurface take.

Even the excitement that follows cannot compare with that first electric moment of the take. It is the ultimate reward of summer, surely one of the best moments of the year.

Birthday Fish

On the morning of my birthday I awoke with a raging sinus headache. I lay in bed a while, hoping the headache would go away, but all it did was move around a little until it found a spot it seemed to like, just to the left of my nose. There it settled down and felt as if it meant to stay.

I had been planning to spend the day on the river. A few days earlier it had been too high to fish, but there had been dry weather since—dry enough to bring the river down to fishing shape. It would be the first chance of the year to try for a summer steelhead.

The thought of a steelhead contended with the headache and the steelhead won. I crawled out of bed, swallowed two cups of coffee and some aspirin, loaded my waders and tackle in the truck and started out for the river.

It was a warm day but not too bright, some fluffy clouds were scattered around the sky and there was a gentle breeze. That much was good, but the headache was persistent; it grew worse as I drove north on the freeway in heavy summer traffic.

The trip took an hour and by the time I reached the river I was feeling sorry I had come. The river looked in shape, as I had thought it would, but a bad sinus headache can destroy your enthusiasm for just about anything—even the chance for a steelhead on the fly.

I sat in the shade, thinking what a lousy way this was to spend a birthday, and waited to see if the pain would go away. After a while it did subside a little, and though I didn't feel quite up to fishing I decided I felt well enough to tie a fly or two. The stock in my steelhead fly boxes was low; it had not been replenished since the last summer season.

I don't know whether any medical authority has ever investigated the therapeutic value of fly tying, but if not then someone should. After a dozen flies had emerged from my vise the headache had vanished and I felt some of my usual vigor starting to return. By then it was late afternoon, the day was cooling and long shadows were beginning to reach out across the stream, but from where I sat I could see my favorite run was empty—I hadn't seen anyone there all day—and that was the last bit of encouragement I needed.

Returning to the truck, I removed the graphite rod from its long tube and joined the sections together, mounted the reel and strung the sinking line through the guides, then took one of the flies I had just tied and knotted it to the end of the leader. I slipped on a pair of stocking-foot waders and laced up the wading shoes, then wriggled into the overloaded vest with its bulging pockets and headed for the river.

I scrambled down the bank, started upstream toward my favorite run and stopped. Another fisherman was just wading in at the head of the run. He moved around a little until he found a spot he seemed to like, just to the left of the tongue of current flowing through the pool. There he settled down and looked as if he meant to stay.

I stood there, muttering single-syllable words, and wondered what to do next. Then I remembered another promising run a little way downstream and decided that it might be worth a look.

The run was empty when I arrived so I waded in and began casting. The water was cool and so was the air above it and both felt good, and soon

I found myself caught up in the gentle rhythm of the river. It was satisfying to be there, to reach out with a long line and drop the fly close to the far shore, then feel the line come alive in the current as it started its downstream swing. But I was hoping for something more than just the feel of the current on the line.

I fished patiently and thoroughly through the run, stopping after each pair of downstream steps to search the water with several casts before I took another pair of steps and stopped to search again. In such methodical fashion I fished almost to the end of the pool—and there, just as a long cast straightened out below, I felt the heavy pull of a steelhead.

Perhaps it was because I was out of practice, or perhaps just because the fish took me by surprise, but for whatever reason I struck too hard. The leader tippet parted like a cobweb.

That brought quite a few more single-syllable words to mind. I was angry and disgusted—not at the fish, but at myself for having missed the chance. There are not so many opportunities to hook a steelhead on the fly that an angler can afford to waste many of them—especially one that falls upon his birthday.

There were no more steelhead waiting in the remainder of the pool and finally I left it and started back, still feeling most unhappy with myself. Wading across the river, I glanced upstream and saw the same angler still planted in my favorite run. That did not make me any less unhappy. Soon it would be too dark to fish, and I faced the specter of a fishless birthday.

Then the other fisherman abruptly reeled in, waded out of the river and vanished into the woods, leaving the empty pool to beckon. Quickly I considered the possibilities: The other fisherman had spent a lot of time in the pool and probably had covered it thoroughly; if he hadn't taken a fish that likely meant there were no fish there to be taken.

Still, there was no harm in trying.

There was not enough light left to fish the full length of the run, so I started in near the tail where I'd always had the best results. Immediately everything went wrong; the fly line came up tangled from the stripping basket, and no sooner had I got it straightened out than it tangled once again. With little patience I plucked at the loops and coils until the line was free and I could cast, but then the leader snarled. Finally exhausting my vocabulary of one-syllable words, I picked through the monofilament maze in the fading light until once again the leader was free of knots, or nearly so.

At last I made a decent cast, then another and a third. The third cast had barely settled to the water when a fish seized the fly. This time I set the hook more gently and the fish reacted slowly, moving out into the center of the run and taking a few turns of line from the reel. It didn't feel especially large, but it was a fish and that was all I wanted.

Then the fish ran strongly, taking the line down into the backing. It jumped at the head of the pool and I could see that it was big and bright. I was well below it, just where I wanted to be, and I recovered line as the fish fought the pressure of both the current and the rod. It ran again and jumped a second time, far out of the water in a graceful parabola. After that we traded line, the fish jumped again, and then I got the upper hand and led it into shallow water. It turned on its side and I thought it was done, but suddenly it turned upright and ran again, the strongest run yet, and took all the line and much of the backing as it headed far upstream.

When the run finally ended I began reeling in as quickly as I could, but it seemed the fly line would never come in view. At last the backing splice came through the guides and several turns of fly line came in on top of it, but then the fish ran again, stopped and thrashed heavily on the surface.

The line went slack. I reeled frantically but there was no answering pull. With growing despair, I kept reeling until all the line was on the reel and the leader butt was showing.

Then I felt the fish again. It had gone around me and was holding just below, almost within my reach. The current had formed a slack belly in the line when the fish made its sudden move, and in the dim evening light I couldn't tell where it had gone.

But now I knew. I went ashore, got below the fish again and steered it close enough so that finally I was able to reach down and give it a gentle shove onto the wet stones along the river's edge.

It was the most beautiful fish I had ever seen—snow white on its belly, bright silver on its sides and gleaming steel-gray on its back, without a single flaw or blemish. Its form was just as flawless—a small head, thick body and powerful tail, every fin shaped perfectly. This was no hatchery fish; only nature could have made a fish as beautiful as this.

I measured it against my rod—29 inches—and guessed its weight at somewhere between eight and nine pounds. Then I carefully removed the fly and lifted the fish gently back into the river, holding it there until it exploded from my grasp and went on about its interrupted way.

I stood again and looked around. The sun had set, bats were feeding on the evening hatch and the day was nearly done.

But I felt good. It was my birthday, and the river had remembered.

Pages from a Trout
Fisherman's Diary

Trout fishermen are known for the diaries they keep. Their journals, dating back almost to the misty origins of the sport, have given us a rich and colorful record of trout fishing through the ages. Few other activities of man have inspired such proliferacy and devotion for so long.

That devotion remains true to this day. In fact, it shows signs of growing—in recent years angling diaries have become more commonplace than ever. But there are signs their purpose may be changing: Many anglers seem to have dismissed the notion of the diary as a personal angling journal and have begun using it instead as a repository for technical information that might have future use. If there is a hatch of pale sulfur duns on a particular river at 2 p.m. on July 11, they record that information faithfully; then, if they should happen to be fishing the same water a year hence, they can look in their diaries and learn what to expect.

Sensing this trend, various entrepreneurs have begun selling printed page forms with neatly arranged columns and spaces in which a trout fisherman can record just about any kind of technical information he could possibly want—water temperature and clarity, hatches observed and the times they began and ended, fly patterns used and results obtained, weather data, trout species caught and the length and weight of each, and so on and on. I suppose such forms have a proper place, but it always has seemed to me they are better suited for accountants than for anglers. Certainly they do nothing to encourage free expression.

It's not that I don't keep detailed records in my own journal, but I do so in my own fashion—and once having recorded the information, I seldom refer to it again. "You can look it up," as Casey Stengel used to say, and I can; but I hardly ever do. For I learned long ago that the best reason for keeping a fishing journal is to preserve the treasured experiences of a fishing lifetime—experiences that might suffer from distortion or disappear if left to the mercies of a frail human memory.

Now I read my journal to relive those moments from the past. Its faded pages bring to mind old names and familiar places and revive the vivid excitement of times gone by. In it I can find the triumphant words I wrote after the capture of my first steelhead, or the joyful account of my first salmon on a fly—along with records of all the unsuccessful trips that led up to those happy days. It holds the description of my first rainbow from Lake Taupo, the story of my first Alaska cutthroat, and the records of countless fish caught in waters close to home. For me, it is the best of all fishing books.

Some of its pages still have trout scales stuck to them, preserved for study under a microscope but serving also as reminders of struggles with memorable fish. Between other pages are copies of old licenses, souvenirs of trips to exotic places; still others bear scribbled maps of routes to obscure waters or notes on the fly patterns that succeeded in them. There are details of a thousand trips, some delightful and others disappointing, but each one worth recording at the time, and worth remembering now.

My diary reminds me that I was fishing in a mountain lake on that historic day in 1969 when men first landed on the moon, and that I caught and released more than 50 lively brook trout before racing home to watch on television as that first giant step was taken for all mankind.

It also brings back to mind my first impression of the mighty Deschutes River in Oregon. "The Deschutes is aptly named," I wrote on that July day in 1973, "a swift-flowing river with many rapids breaking over lava ledges and great boulders. It is different from any river I have fished before—a wide, mostly shallow stream that carries a good amount of glacial silt . . . The walls of its canyon are spectacular basalt terraces and turrets, and the river is lined with trees of sparse foliage, all flat-topped from the wind. It is a strange country, both friendly and forbidding, and I am glad for a chance to see it. . . ."

Reading that now, I can see it all again—as well as everything that followed: "We went up about 12 miles and began fishing at 6:15 a.m. By 7 the sun was over the rim of the canyon, but it never did become too warm—though the sky was clear—because the river itself was cool and a strong wind came up with the sun . . . I went without a fish until about 2 p.m. At that time I was fishing a drift right below an abandoned railroad water tower, using a No. 6 Skunk, which is about all I used all day. Suddenly the fly was taken by a strong fish that took me about 200 yards downstream in a series of short rushes before I beached it—a fine bright buck steelhead of about 25 or 26 inches and around seven pounds—a very solid, block-shaped fish."

Two months later I was in British Columbia fishing for Kamloops trout, and my diary holds the record of a remarkable sight on a wilderness lake: "Two large bears standing upright, grappling and wrestling in the water. They began to roll around and kick spray at each other and appeared to be having as much fun as a couple of kids in a water fight." I watched them for a long time, and I remember wondering if man's traditional view of bears as dangerous animals might be wrong; perhaps I was witnessing a display of their true nature.

Those preprinted diary forms offer no space for observations such as that.

A year later I returned to British Columbia to make a fishing film for a network television program. The network had chosen Peter Duchin, the famous band leader, to be the "featured fisherman" and I was to be his guide. Each of us was "wired" for sound and kept under the unwavering eye of a camera while we tried to coax trout to floating flies.

My journal tells the story: On the first day "a few sedges were on the water, but no fish were rising. We fished seriously for an hour or an hour and a half without result . . . I could not help but feel badly that we caught nothing, but apparently the film crew is used to this sort of thing. I hope the lake is cooperative tomorrow; I feel the pressure to produce results."

Next day was a little better: "Shortly before noon, the traveling sedges started coming off in good numbers and the fish started rising. I rose one and broke it and Peter rose two and broke both of them. Then I rose and hooked a fish of about 2½ pounds and landed it—our first fish on camera." But the effort was for naught: "The noise of cattle and the appearance of many other boats soured the camera crew."

It was a busy week. We were up early each morning for breakfast and the long drive to the lake that we had chosen for the filming. Then we would fish and film all day—work which turned out to be much more difficult than I'd ever imagined it would be—and drive back for a late dinner at the lodge where we were staying. After dinner I would usually stay up until the early hours of the next morning, tying flies for use in the day's fishing or talking with members of the film crew.

The fishing never was very good, but the trout cooperated just often enough for the camera crew to get what it had come for—and our six days of fishing eventually were condensed to 12 minutes of film shown on the network.

When the work finally was done and the director pronounced himself satisfied, there was still one day left to fish for fun. And on that day my journal says we found "the finest hatch of traveling sedges I have ever seen . . . I rose and hooked a fine trout that jumped several times, took line and gave an excellent account of itself before I finally landed it. It was the best fish of the week—and, of course, better than any we filmed on the show."

Later that summer I visited the little upper Gibbon in Yellowstone Park. "The river is hardly more than a brook at this point, meandering through a lush meadow," I wrote. It was full of small brook trout—"and, much to my surprise, a 14-inch, 1¼-pound rainbow."

My journal rekindles the memory of that fish: I had fished upstream through the meadow to the point where a highway bridge spans the creek, and by then I had nearly given up hope of finding any sizable fish in that tiny stream. I was ready to leave when I heard a heavy splash under the bridge.

The meadow was bright with sunshine, but under the bridge it was pitch dark in the shade. I listened for a while and the splash came again. There was no way to see what was causing it but I guessed it might be a trout, feeding somewhere back in the shadows. So I stripped line from the reel, stood well back from the bridge and pitched my little dry fly far up into the darkness underneath. The current brought slack line back to me and I gathered it in and waited until I heard the splash again. Then I struck.

A large rainbow came tumbling out of the darkness into the sunshine, and it was hard to tell which of us was more surprised. The fish's size and strength were far out of proportion to the stream, but it fought as hard as the close quarters would allow. When it finally came trembling to my grasp I released it quickly and carefully, then watched as it headed swiftly back for its dark lair beneath the bridge. I wonder now if its descendants still sip flies in the shadows of that little bridge.

There are many entries from Hosmer Lake in my diary, simply because I have fished for the transplanted Atlantic salmon there so often and so long. There is one about a salmon that jumped into the boat and just as promptly jumped out again, another that recalls the time an osprey plunged from the sky and tried to catch a fish I was playing and another about the time an otter seized a fish right beneath my fly.

It also was at Hosmer where my backcast once hooked a nighthawk on the wing. My diary reports what happened next: "After what can only be described as a very interesting fight—or flight—with the line wound twice around my spare rod and once under the outboard motor shaft, I got the bird to the side of the boat, where I could see it was hooked near the base of one wing. By then it was angry—no doubt about that—and it opened its mouth and said 'Scrawwk!' With a healthy respect for its talons and beak, I broke off about 30 inches of tippet and the bird flew off with my No. 16 Blue Upright still stuck in its wing.

"Well, after all, this is supposed to be a catch-and-release lake."

A few days later my friend Dave Draheim also accidentally hooked a nighthawk. This one flew in circles, trussing up Dave in four turns of his own fly line—one of the funniest sights I have seen in all my years of fishing.

Of all the Hosmer Lake entries in my diary, my favorite is one written on the last day of a long stay:

"The morning dawned cold with a solid overcast and a threat of rain. More or less as a pilgrimage, I went to the upper lake, not really expecting to find anything there. The wind was cold and cruel and Mount Bachelor and the stately South Sister lay hidden in the lowering mists. But all the other familiar sights were there—the moss-covered snag on the point beyond the lava reef, the tules bending and bowing gracefully in the wind, the withered pines in the encroaching meadow around the lake. Ospreys and eagles floated overhead against the dark backdrop of the sky and when the wind died momentarily I could hear birdsongs from the meadow, mixed with an occasional whistling flight of ducks. Even in the cold, gray light of this somber day, Hosmer is a magical place, a place of wild and magnificent beauty.

"And while taking it all in, I searched also for the elusive dark shadows of salmon moving beneath the waves. The usual haunts seemed empty of fish, so I drifted on the wind, past the point with the old snag, past the mouth of the little lagoon where last year I went swimming on a hot, still day, and on to the next point with its short skirt of dark lava rocks where, every once in a great while, I have found the salmon gathered and feeding.

"And they were there again today, rising and boiling in the rough, wind-whipped water. Quickly I was fast to one, an angry salmon flashing away on its first fierce run, then jumping high and throwing a burst of spray into the wind. Then came a long struggle of give and take, the salmon taking line in shrill bursts from the little Hardy reel, then yielding sullenly to the pressure as I regained the line. After several shorter runs and two or three more tumbling jumps, we approached the end game—two determined players, each making careful moves, each trying to avoid a fatal error that would result in loss of the game. For the salmon, the stakes were his life, for he could not know that I would let him keep it. And when his last energy ebbed and he came alongside in obedience to the spring of the rod, I twisted the fly free and the salmon knew that he had won as well as lost.

"Throughout the long, cold, windy afternoon the salmon came, sometimes in quick succession. I raised many more than I could hook because the wind was unrelenting, blowing wide bellies in the line so that I couldn't set the hook before the quick salmon was gone. And late in the day the wind blew hard pellets of rain onto my glasses as I fought a last strong fish that ran twice into the backing and gave me a long, stirring fight before I twisted the fly free and restored him to the lake.

"And when it was finally over, I had felt the weight of 26 salmon on my line, 15 of which I landed. In addition, there was a single plump brook trout.

"So another fine year at Hosmer Lake is over. It has become so much a highlight of my year that I think of it often during the long days of winter work. I hope it will be here, waiting, for as long as I am able to come, and for my children after me."

It is still there, waiting, although the fishing has declined sadly in recent years. I hope it will soon be restored and that Hosmer Lake will yet account for many more pages in my diary.

Over the years my diary has grown to fill 28 notebooks and I am just now starting number 29. Many hours and much work have gone into those pages, but "it was an employment for his idle time, which was then not idly spent," as Izaak Walton once succinctly said. It also has been time spent in the most pleasant way, transcribing adventures as they happened, then reading and re-reading about them later.

I do not know or really care if anyone else will ever read what is written in these notebooks, but I do know they have always pleased their intended audience of one. If someone else should read them, I suppose they would seem less interesting to him than they have always seemed to me. But if he had the patience to keep reading, he would find the account of one fishing trip that was extraordinary by any standards—a trip that literally became a voyage into the twilight zone. It is the entry dated May 18, 1980.

On that bright spring Sunday morning I had taken my family to Dry Falls Lake in eastern Washington. We arrived early, just as a tremendous dragonfly hatch was getting under way. Dozens of big, stubby nymphs had crawled out of the lake and up onto dry land, leaving awkward trails as they crossed the dusty road to the grass on the far side. There they climbed the stalks and began the slow process of extracting themselves from their nymphal shucks. The children went to watch this curious pilgrimage while Joan, my wife, set up a camp stove to heat the morning coffee and I made preparations to go fishing.

The coffee perked and added its pleasant scent to the fresh morning air and we were just about to take the first sip when the sounds came. At first there was only a gentle ripple in the air, so soft and subtle I was uncertain I had heard anything at all. Then it came again, much louder this time, a deep, ominous rumble that grew in volume until it became a mighty swell of sound that washed against the coulee walls, echoing and re-echoing around the great amphitheater of the Dry Falls.

The children were frightened and came running to ask what was happening, but I had no explanation to offer. The sound was not thunder or a sonic boom, nor did it seem possible it could have carried from the Army's Yakima Firing Range; it was too far away. Then I had a joking thought: "Maybe Mount St. Helens blew her top," I said. The children laughed, reassured that I could jest, and soon returned to their play.

The sound faded as abruptly as it had come and we soon forgot it. I started fishing about 9:30 a.m.; the dragonfly hatch had ended, but within an hour the damselfly nymphs began to move and fish started rising. Four good rainbows came to my fly and fought well, giving me a difficult time in the weedy shallows. It was a good morning, passing quickly as all good mornings do.

It was nearly noon when I glanced over my shoulder and noticed for the first time an ominous dark cloud spreading over the coulee rim from south and east. It looked like a big thunderstorm headed our way, and remembering the violence of some other storms I'd experienced at Dry Falls, I knew it would be a good idea to seek cover before it hit. Perhaps I could go ashore and have lunch, then wait for the storm to pass and resume fishing in the afternoon.

I made a few more casts, then started for shore, keeping a wary eye on the approaching cloud. It seemed to be moving in quickly, though the lake was still strangely calm and trout were still rising.

Other fishermen also were heading for shelter. Most loaded up their gear and left, and we sat and ate our lunch and watched them go until only one or two remained. The dark cloud now covered half the sky.

I walked up the road to the top of the first rise where I could look south along the coulee. The cloud extended for as far as I could see; it was a big storm, one that looked as if it would last at least throughout the afternoon. Reluctantly, I decided we should pack up and follow the others who had left.

I told Joan and the children to gather up their things while I put away my rods and hoisted my little pram atop the truck. We worked quickly, expecting the storm to strike at any moment, but though it grew ever darker there was still no wind, nor yet a hint of rain.

It was completely dark by the time we were ready to leave—not just storm-dark or twilight-dark, but as dark as the deepest, blackest night. The cloud had filled the sky, stretching from one rim of the coulee to the other, and it had completely swallowed up the day. All the familiar landmarks of the Dry Falls had disappeared and we were surrounded instead by vague shapes and masses that we felt rather than saw. Even the noisy yellow-headed and redwing blackbirds in the tules around the lakeshore had suddenly grown still.

It was 1 o'clock in the afternoon, but it was night.

I started the truck, switched on the headlights and shifted into low gear for the first hill on the tortuous, rocky road out of the Dry Falls. By this time only one other fisherman remained and he also was working hurriedly to load his boat and leave. He looked anxiously at the sky as we drove slowly past. "I've never seen anything like this," he said.

Neither had we.

By the time we had driven a quarter of a mile the darkness had become so murky and impenetrable that even the high beams of the truck's headlights could scarcely drill a thin tunnel of light ahead of us. Then I noticed a thick, heavy mist floating in the headlights and beginning to collect on the windshield. The storm was at last beginning.

"Here comes the rain," I said.

"That isn't rain," Joan said quietly. She was right. Whatever it was, it was dry.

The bright morning, so full of promise, had dissolved into total, impenetrable darkness. And now something was falling from the sky and it wasn't rain. We could see nothing, except for the pair of ruts that appeared dimly in the headlights, and hear nothing, except for the truck's engine straining to overcome the grade. It was as if we had made a wrong turn to another planet, or had suddenly crossed the threshold of a forbidden dimension.

There had to be some rational explanation and I could think of only one: That Mount St. Helens *had* exploded, with more cataclysmic force than anyone could ever possibly have imagined.

"Turn on the radio," Joan said. "There must be something on the radio." I hadn't turned it on before because reception is difficult down in the rocky pocket of the Dry Falls. But I did so now.

There was lightning in the air. It crashed and crackled across the radio band as I dialed, searching for a station. There were snatches of faint, far-off music, blurred by static. And then the frightened voice of a disc jockey at a station in nearby Moses Lake: "Mount St. Helens has erupted and ash is falling everywhere in the Columbia Basin. All roads in the area are closed. If you're in a car, pull over and stop!"

The voice was near panic; the disc jockey obviously was having as much trouble coping with the situation as we were. And yet his voice was somehow comforting, a link to the familiar world that had disappeared so suddenly an hour before. And it confirmed the explanation for the explosions we had heard and for our present plight.

But I was not about to take the disc jockey's advice. Pulling over and stopping was the last thing I wanted to do. Ash from the exploded volcano was falling thickly outside the truck; already I could smell and taste the stuff and it made my throat dry. It might be toxic. If we stopped, it seemed possible we might not be able to go on breathing in the gritty atmosphere. I decided to try to get away from this phantom rain and ugly darkness as quickly as I could, back to someplace where the air was clear and it was light.

It was a strange ride out of the Dry Falls, with the windshield wipers working to keep the ash from piling up and the headlights illuminating a dim path through the darkness that had come up out of the earth. But finally the rocky ruts gave way to a narrow band of asphalt that led southwest toward the nearest highway, and eventually we found ourselves in a line of other cars fleeing from the cloud. Each car stirred up an enormous roostertail of blinding dust that forced those behind to slow or stop until it settled.

In such halting fashion we made it to the highway and turned north, crawling through the dusty darkness until the headlights dimly picked out the sign for the junction with U.S. Highway 2, the route westward to the Cascades. If we went that way, I hoped, perhaps we could escape the cloud; we might even be able to make it over the mountains to our home in Seattle.

For 10 or 20 minutes we drove slowly westward in darkness. Then, far ahead, a dull gleam of light appeared, low on the horizon as if it were shining under the hem of a curtain. It grew larger and brighter as we continued toward it. The announcer at a radio station in Wenatchee assured us that Highway 2 was closed, but we kept on going.

Soon it was bright enough to see beyond the cone of light from the truck headlights. Everything was gray; ash swirled on the highway like new-fallen powder snow and filled the furrows of the plowed fields along the road. I thought about the ash being sucked into the truck's air intake and worried that it would choke the carburetor and kill the engine, but the truck plowed ahead steadily into the storm of ash.

It was sometime after 3 when we reached Wenatchee. The sun was a sullen glow in a dusty sky and thick ash and dust were blowing in the streets, but still it was a scene that seemed infinitely hospitable compared to the one we had left at Dry Falls. We had come from darkness into light, traversing a dusty moonscape which only that morning had been lush with green grass, freshly plowed dark rows of earth and trees filled with ripening fruit.

From Wenatchee we drove into the mountains toward Stevens Pass, soon leaving the last of the ash behind us. The sky again brightened to a faultless blue and afternoon sunlight glinted from the silvery caps of late spring snow still clinging to the Cascade peaks. We breathed cool, clean air and gave silent thanks.

In another two hours we were home.

We were lucky. Thousands of others were not so fortunate. They were stranded for days in tiny, ash-choked towns or roadside rest areas, forced to a halt by blinding, blowing ash or by car engines that choked to death on the noxious stuff.

We also were lucky in another way: We had witnessed the awesome power of nature in a way that few people ever have. Those in other parts of the world who read of the explosion of Mount St. Helens in newspapers or watched it on television will never comprehend the full magnitude of the event; even the most powerful descriptive phrases or the most startling photographs cannot convey it properly. In order to understand how big—how incredible—it really was, you had to see it for yourself.

Now my vision of it is preserved in the pages of my fishing diary, along with the accounts of many less eventful days. It is there among the yellowing licenses, scribbled maps and fly patterns and the pages with trout scales still stuck to them—each one a separate record of some adventure from the past.

And that, I think, is the true test of what a trout fisherman's diary ought to be—not how much information it can hold, but how well it preserves the memories of a fishing lifetime and reminds a man of all the fun he's had.

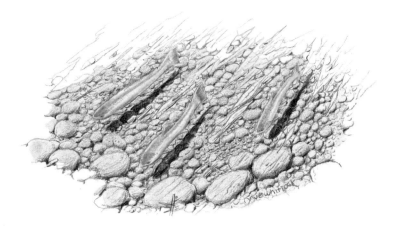

The Once and Future River

The Green was only a little river, a mere capillary in the giant circulatory system that feeds the great Columbia. It emerged quietly from between high timbered ridges in the south Cascades, and all through the long summers it carried away the snowmelt in a gently diminishing flow.

Winter was a different story. In winter the river often shed its quiet personality and sometimes flooded violently, and the torrents would change it so that when anglers returned in the spring they could never be certain what they would find. The Green was a river one had to learn again and again.

But it was a river well worth learning. Despite its diminutive size and distance from the sea, it drew into itself large runs of bright steelhead in the summer and handsome sea-run cutthroat in the fall. It had salmon, too, a big early-autumn run that returned to a hatchery near the river's mouth. From the eve of summer to the twilight of the fall, an angler could always find fish in the Green.

There are dozens of rivers named Green, perhaps scores. Some are large; some, like this one, small. Only a few are actually green. This one was not—at least I never saw it so. Maybe it was once, back before loggers cut the giant firs that grew along its banks; back then it might have reflected the soft, deep green of fir boughs that stretched across its narrow width. But all trees of that stature were long gone by the time I got to know the Green, replaced by a host of maples, cottonwoods and alders and a new generation of firs not yet tall enough to be reflected in the stream. Perhaps if one looked into the depths of the river's largest, deepest pools he could have seen a hint of green, but I will always remember the Green as a silver-colored river, sparkling and lively and full of highlights in the bright summer sunshine.

It also was a generous river, easily waded and easily fished. In most places it took only a gentle roll cast to cover the most promising water with a fly, and often in the low water of late summer the steelhead would be plainly visible—sleek, silver-gray shapes lying in the hollows between boulders in the tailwaters of the pools. It was necessary to be cautious in order to see them without them seeing you first, and I remember spending a long time crawling through the brush to the edge of a pool, then cautiously raising my head to see if a fish was there.

If one was, the next problem was to find a way to put a fly over it without causing it to take alarm. Sometimes the solution was to go back through the woods and well upstream, then wade out cautiously, hunched over, and make a sidearm cast with a long sinking line and let the river carry the fly down to the fish. Or sometimes the answer was to go downstream and approach the fish from below, casting up with a long line and a big high-floating dry fly. Sometimes, no matter what you did, the fish would sense your presence and vanish so quickly it would leave you wondering if you had ever really seen it at all. But every now and then things would go just right, the cast would fall on target and the fish would take the fly.

It's hard for a steelhead to show all its strength in a small river, but the Green River fish always did the best they could—and often that was enough to leave you breathless and trembling, with a broken leader, a lost fly and shattered hopes. But again there were times when all would go well, when the tackle would hold despite the best efforts of the fish, and a long fight would end with a bright steelhead on the beach. Those were the times that made the Green a steelheader's favorite—my favorite.

The first time I went there was with Joe Pierce and Enos Bradner, two river-wise old veterans who had spent more years chasing steelhead than I had been alive. It was good to have such men as teachers, and I watched and listened to them carefully as we explored the river from the salmon hatchery downstream to the enormous pool where it joined the larger North Fork of the Toutle. It was late July and the water was low and we soon found three fish shifting nervously in the shallow tail-out of a riffle. We took turns casting to them but only Bradner could solicit one to strike. The fish followed his fly and took it hard, but the connection was only momentary before the fly came free. After that the fish ignored our offerings.

We finished the day without catching any fish, but the chance to see the river was reward enough for me. It was an intriguing little river, large enough to hold big fish but small enough to share its secrets, and I found myself wanting to return. Soon enough I did so, and that was the beginning of a long friendship with the Green.

It was not until my third trip that I hooked my first steelhead. It happened in a long pool on the lower river, a fine stretch of wrinkled water with good depth and plenty of places for fish to hold. I found nothing in the upper half of the pool, but midway through a fish took my fly solidly, ran hard and jumped twice, revealing itself as a bright summer steelhead of perhaps 10 pounds. I was afraid the fish would run out of the pool into the rapids down below, but it suddenly changed direction, dashed upstream the full length of the pool and jumped again, far out of the water in a somersaulting leap. It fell back with a crash, then darted into the remains of an old log jam and broke the leader somewhere in the jackstraw tangle of waterlogged limbs. It happened so quickly that I scarcely had time to draw a breath, but I still remember the sight of that great silver fish hovering over the water at the apex of its final leap.

Early that evening I returned to the same pool and hooked another fish, a smaller one. This time the contest went my way and when it was over I had captured my first Green River steelhead—a handsome fish that glowed softly silver in the mother-of-pearl light of a rising full moon.

I grew to love that pool. My private name for it was the Long Pool, simply because it was the longest of all the pools I fished on the river. It began where the river made a narrow right-angle turn, skirting the edge of the log jam where the first fish had broken me, and then it widened out and flowed along a gravel bar that offered ample backcast room. On the far bank was a big alder whose shadow would fall across the pool on summer afternoons; usually it wasn't long before a fish moved into the shadow, and I discovered I could go there each day with the almost certain knowledge that a steelhead would be waiting. It was the closest thing to clockwork fishing that I've ever seen.

Once I hooked a fish on my first cast into the shadow. The steelhead jumped once, then ran out of the pool into the rapids down below and took my line around a rock. I followed it down and waded out cautiously in the fast water until I found the rock and freed the line. The fish ran again, this time across the river to a spot where the current had eaten into the bank and left a tree leaning dangerously with one limb trailing in the current. There the fish jumped again and carried my leader over the limb.

There was nothing to do but try to wade across and free the leader. The current was strong and the rocks were slippery, so I took my time and chose each foothold carefully until at last I reached the trailing limb. I stripped away the leaves and removed the leader. Once it was free the fish ran again.

So far the fight had gone all the fish's way, but now it made its first mistake. Its run carried it downstream, out of the rapids into a quiet pool, and for the first time I began to think I might have a chance to land it. But first I had to wade all the way back across the river, through the same fast water and over the same slippery rocks, trying to remember where I'd put my feet on the first crossing. It was a near thing, but I made it without falling, scrambled up onto the bank and dashed downstream to the next pool, where the fish was rushing around busily. Finally it was too tired to resist any longer and I steered it safely to a patch of sandy beach. It was a bright eight-pounder, far from the largest steelhead I'd ever caught, but it had put up one of the longest, toughest fights I'd ever had from any fish.

The Long Pool was more than generous all that first summer, but the next winter a flood gnawed away its lower end and filled in part of its head and after that it wasn't such a long pool any more. But the big alder survived the flood and still gave its shade on summer afternoons, and for another year the steelhead still sought shelter there. Then came another winter and another flood that took the alder and all that remained of the pool.

It was a loss the river never quite replaced, though there were other good pools and it was seldom one could not find a fish in at least one of them. Once I found one holding in the tail-out of the very last pool in the river, just above the Toutle. The fish stood out in bold relief in the low, clear water, and it must have been able to see me as clearly as I could see it. But after I stood and watched it for a while it seemed to accept me as a normal part of things and showed no alarm when I began to cast.

After a few casts I was able to gauge the current and distance well enough to swing my fly within inches of the fish's snout, but the steelhead eyed each offering stoically and made no move. I began changing flies after each half-dozen casts, alternating size and color, and went on casting until the fish finally began to display some little signs of interest. At first these were no more than subtle movements of the fins, repeated each time the fly transcribed its arc past the fish's nose. Then the steelhead suddenly shifted to its left and half-turned toward the fly. But its pursuit was brief and ended without a take, and the fish settled back in its familiar lie.

I sensed the fish had grown excited, but so had I and my fingers trembled as I changed the fly one more time.

Once more I made the familiar cast. Two pairs of anxious eyes— mine and the fish's—followed the fly as it settled just under the surface and began its semicircular swing. I thought I was ready for what would happen next, but the steelhead attacked the fly so savagely it nearly pulled the rod from my grasp. In the split second it took me to recover, the fish let go of the fly.

It was hard to believe a fish could hit so hard and escape without being hooked, but that is what had happened. I couldn't see where it had gone, but after a while I found it again, lying between two boulders a little way downstream. I resumed casting, but this time there was no sign of interest; it was clear the fish could not be tempted a second time.

By then it was nearly dark and time to go. I reeled in and started up the trail, heading into evening gloom that was no deeper than my own.

But such disappointments were more the exception than the rule, and over the years I built up a store of many happy memories of the Green. There were pleasant trips with Ralph Wahl, Ted Rogowski, Ray Kotrla, Alan Pratt, Errol Champion, and Ward McClure; there was the time we found wild blackberries ripe on the Fourth of July and ended up eating baked steelhead and wild blackberry pie, and there were many morning walks along the dusty road that paralleled the river, always cool in the shade of the leafy woods.

Now those memories are all that remain, for the Green River as I knew it is no more. It vanished forever on that tragic May morning when Mount St. Helens unleashed her devastating wrath.

In those first few flaming moments the volcano's blast reached out over the ridgetops and down into the headwaters of the Green, searing trees with its heat and flattening them with its incredible force. A great steaming mudflow raced down the Toutle's North Fork and carried away everything in its path. The mud filled in the junction pool and pushed up the lower Green, burying half a mile of river and the hatchery that had kept it filled with salmon in the fall. Whatever was spared by blast and mud was covered by a steady rain of ash.

A month after the eruption I went looking for the Green. The area was closed to entry because of continuing danger from the simmering volcano so my search was from a plane. It was a sad, strange flight over an alien landscape. Nothing was familiar; all the old landmarks were gone or changed beyond recognition.

Finally I found the remains of the river. Its headwaters were choked with downed timber and cloaked in ash. A narrow band of dirty gray-white water oozed between its banks, flowing past the corpses of a thousand fallen trees to vanish somewhere in the sea of muck that filled the river's lower end. It was a dead river, flowing through a dead land. I flew home sadly, feeling as if I had just come from the funeral of an old friend.

Nature works slowly, but in time it will cleanse and heal the river. Many years from now a new generation of firs will grow up to stretch their limbs across the Green and shade the mountain slopes so that the snow again will slowly melt and fuel the river with a steady cold clear flow. Perhaps wary summer steelhead will pause again to rest in sheltered pools and anglers once more will cast their flies in the bright riffles of the Green. My son may be among them, but the Green will never heal in time for me.

Yet I feel no envy for those anglers of the future, for I remember the Green River as it was.

Hello Dolly!

Most trout have names that are at least suggestive of their nature. The rainbow, cutthroat, and brown trout all were named for their appearance, the steelhead's name tells something about both its color and its disposition, and the common name for the Eastern brook trout gives a pretty good idea of where it might be found. But there's one fish whose name doesn't fit the pattern: The Dolly Varden.

Of course the Dolly Varden is not a true trout, but it looks enough like one that most anglers call it a trout, and it shares waters occupied by both trout and salmon. Unlike those fish, however, the Dolly Varden isn't one that wealthy industrialists or beer barons would travel a thousand miles to catch before retiring for cocktails on the veranda of a private lodge. The Dolly Varden is a fish with few followers or friends.

Yet there are some anglers who fish for Dolly Varden; they've found it a useful fall-back fish when trout are scarce or unwilling. But they generally keep quiet about it, because being a Dolly Varden fisherman is not something you'd want to admit in polite company. That's because most high-minded trout fishermen think of the Dolly Varden as a fish with a five o'clock shadow and a blackjack in its pocket, the kind of fish you wouldn't want to meet after dark. In their view, Dolly Varden might make a good name for a motorcycle gang.

The object of all this contempt is actually a char, a member of the genus *Salvelinus*, a close kin of the Arctic char, a cousin of the Eastern brook trout and lake trout and a distant cousin of the true trouts. It dwells in rivers and lakes of the Pacific Coast from the Aleutian Islands through Alaska and as far south as northern California, and reaches inland through parts of Nevada, Idaho, and Montana into British Columbia and Alberta. There are numerous sea-going populations throughout the northern part of its range, but they do not migrate long distances like steelhead or salmon. Instead, they mostly hang around estuaries, waiting to mug any small fish or other unsuspecting prey that may happen along.

Dolly Varden are similar in color to other chars. Their backs are dark green, sometimes with faint worm-track vermiculations, and their flanks are pale yellow or olive with distinctive scattered red and yellow spots. The leading edges of their pectoral and ventral fins are white, though less so than the ivory etchings on a brook trout's fins. Sea-run fish invariably are bright silver with only faint red and yellow spots.

The Dolly Varden is not wary or graceful like a trout; it's a voracious feeder, a vacuum cleaner of riverbottoms. It gobbles up the eggs of salmon and steelhead and their hatching fry as well. It even has been known to eat shrews, mice, moles, frogs, and small birds. It is extremely vulnerable to all angling methods, especially bait and spoons. It is often caught by steelhead fishermen, but despite its fearsome predatory habits its fight pales in comparison with the steelhead or any other trout. The Dolly Varden rarely jumps, preferring instead to fight in a series of short rushes. Dolly Varden of two to five pounds are common and fish of more than 10 pounds are not exceptional in Alaskan waters, and though fish of such size will put a healthy bend in any rod, they seldom fight as long or as hard as their size would indicate they should.

During past episodes of taxonomic confusion the Dolly Varden was known variously as *Salvelinus spectabilis, S. confluentus, S. bairdii, S. parkei* and *S. campbelli* until general agreement finally was reached on the name *Salvelinus malma*. But in 1978, Ted M. Cavender of the Museum of Zoology at Ohio State University proposed that *S. malma* actually was two different species with overlapping distribution. He revived the name *S. confluentus* for the second species and suggested the common name "bull trout," which somehow seemed more fitting.

Cavender's findings were based on analysis of characteristics of fish taken at many different locations. Those characteristics which distinguish the bull trout from the Dolly Varden include "a long, broad head which is flat above and sharply tapered through the snout," large jaws and teeth and heavy jaw muscles. Cavender concluded the bigger jaws, teeth and muscles were all the better to eat other fish with; in other words, they were the result of piscivorous dietary habits. The bull trout was even more of a fish-eater than the Dolly Varden.

The bull trout is present in some coastal drainages, but the heart of its natural range is inland along the Cascade Range and the Rocky Mountains. It also extends east of the Continental Divide in Canada to the headwaters of the South and North Saskatchewan rivers and the Athabaska, Peace and Liard rivers. Cavender suggests the species may have originated in the Columbia Basin because it is widely distributed there and because that basin borders on the other river basins where it is found.

Cavender's findings have been widely accepted by taxonomists, but few anglers have yet to hear of the new species. When they do, many will discover they have been fishing for bull trout all these years when they thought they were fishing for Dolly Varden.

Not that names or taxomonic differences matter much to casual fishermen. The early white settlers called the Dolly Varden a "red-spotted salmon trout," which would have been an eminently sensible and descriptive name were it not for the fact that the Dolly is neither a salmon nor a trout. The Nisqually Indians got along fine calling it the Pus-sutch; so did the Klallams, who named it Com-mah-mah.

And where did the name Dolly Varden come from? Dolly Varden was a leading character in Charles Dickens' novel, *Barnaby Rudge*, a sort of Victorian *femme fatale* who left a trail of broken hearts through 72 chapters. To quote Dickens:

"When and where was there ever such a plump, roguish, comely, bright-eyed, enticing, bewitching, captivating, maddening little puss in all this world, as Dolly! . . . How many coachmakers, saddlers, cabinet-makers, and professors of other useful arts, had deserted their fathers, mothers, sisters, brothers, and, most of all, their cousins, for the love of her! . . . How many young men, in all previous times of unprecedented steadiness, had turned suddenly wild and wicked for the same reason, and, in an ecstacy of unrequited love, taken to wrench off door-knockers and invert the boxes of rheumatic watchmen! How had she recruited the king's service, both by sea and land, through rendering desperate his loving subjects between the ages of eighteen and twenty-five! How many young ladies had publicly professed, with tears in their eyes, that for their tastes she was much too short, too tall, too bold, too cold, too stout, too thin, too fair, too dark—too everything but handsome! How many old ladies, taking counsel together, had thanked Heaven their daughters were not like her, and had hoped she might come to no harm, and had thought she would come to no good. . . . " But you get the idea.

What has all this got to do with a fish? That's a complicated story. To quote Dickens again:

"As to Dolly, there she was again, the very pink and pattern of good looks, in a smart little cherry-coloured mantle, with a hood of the same drawn over her head, and upon the top of that hood, a little straw hat trimmed with cherry-coloured ribbons, and worn the merest trifle on one side—just enough in short to make it the wickedest and most provoking head-dress that ever malicious milliner devised." When Dickens toured the United States sometime after publication of *Barnaby Rudge*, Dolly Varden hats became all the rage, and one of the most popular was a calico pattern with pink spots. According to legend, some fashion-conscious young lady was shown a freshly caught char with prominent pink spots and promptly exclaimed that it was a regular "Dolly Varden trout." The name stuck, and the Dolly Varden became the only fish ever named after a hat.

It also would be hard to find a more misleading name for a fish. It's not that the Dolly Varden isn't a handsome fish; it's just that it has such a reputation for nasty habits. At one time there was even a widespread notion that the Dolly Varden's habit of eating fish eggs and small fish posed a threat to the survival of salmon and steelhead runs. Overlooking the fact that salmon and steelhead somehow had managed to survive thousands of years despite the predatory habits of the Dolly Varden, anglers began a sort of informal campaign to eradicate the species. Since it was an easy fish to catch, it was caught and killed in wholesale quantities, and logging-camp inhabitants frequently joined in the fun by dynamiting pools where Dolly Varden were known to congregate. It wasn't long before the Dolly Varden became relatively scarce in coastal rivers south of the Canadian border.

But these days, when even the snail darter is grudgingly conceded a right to life, there is a somewhat more benevolent attitude toward the Dolly Varden. Its numbers are gradually increasing and some anglers even have begun to consign to it a sporting value, especially when there aren't any steelhead around—as increasingly there aren't.

My first encounter with a Dolly Varden came while I was dry-fly fishing for steelhead in the North Fork of the Stillaguamish River. The fly had just touched down after a long cast across a pool when a six-inch steelhead smolt rose and took it. Immediately I gave slack in hopes the little fish would not hook itself, but a gentle tugging on the line signaled that it had. I started stripping line rapidly, hoping to bring in the fish and release it as quickly as possible but not paying very much attention to it. Suddenly there was a much stronger pull on the line.

Looking down through the clear water, I was amazed to see that I was fast to a fish at least four times longer than the one that had taken my fly, a fish that was twisting and turning powerfully in the current through the pool. Slowly I played it until I could see its jaws were clamped around the six-inch smolt that had risen to the fly. I fought the fish until it was within arm's length, and only then did it grudgingly release its grip and swim past me, almost brushing against my waders. I could see then that it was a big, mean-looking Dolly Varden, obviously disappointed at having had to give up what it had thought would be an easy meal. For me, the incident confirmed all the unpleasant things I'd heard about this fish.

The first Dolly Varden I actually caught also was while I was fishing for steelhead in the Stillaguamish. My fly was taken at the tail of a riffle by a strong fish that ran well and I thought surely it was a good steelhead. But the fish turned and came to the surface at the end of its run and I caught a glimpse of green and gold and knew immediately it was not a steelhead. It proved to be a fat Dolly Varden whose uncharacteristically vigorous fight was due to the fact that my hook had found a place in its dorsal fin rather than its mouth.

At first I was disgusted, but as I eased the fish up onto the stones of the riverbank the sunlight struck full upon its side and I realized what a handsome fish it was. I understood then how it could have been named after a calico hat with a cluster of pink spots. I gently removed the fly from its dorsal fin and returned the fish carefully to the stream.

Since then I have caught Dolly Varden all the way to Alaska, where they are extremely numerous and still sometimes regarded as something of a nuisance. I've even coaxed a few fresh sea-run Dollys to rise to a dry fly, although such a delicate and esoteric act seems against their general principles.

The Dolly Varden never will be my favorite fish, but it has its own place in the river and its presence has saved me from some blank days. It never will match the speed and power of a steelhead or the stamina of a cutthroat, but nowadays it is something of a bonus to find the Dolly Varden in rivers where once it was so scarce. And in these days of ever more fishermen and fewer fish, it is slowly becoming a target species in its own right. Perhaps someday someone will even write a book about Dolly Varden the fish instead of Dolly Varden the flirt.

Which brings us back to the *other* Dolly Varden, in case you were wondering whatever happened to her: She had a few bad moments, but came through them all unscathed and ended up marrying a poor fellow named Joe, who long before had given up all hope of winning her. They lived happily ever after, and as Dickens wrote: "Go to Chigwell when you would, there would surely be seen, either in the village street, or on the green, or frolicking in the farm-yard . . . more small Joes and small Dollys than could easily be counted."

Truth sometimes imitates fiction, and now in the rivers of the Northwest you will again find more small Dollys—and some bigger ones—than could easily be counted. And some people think it's nice to see the Dolly back where it belongs.

Bucktail Camp

A dozen years ago, in *The Year of the Angler*, I wrote at some length about the history of the North Fork of the Stillaguamish, most celebrated of all Northwest steelhead rivers. Much of the lore and many of the techniques of steelhead fly fishing were developed on the North Fork, and virtually every famous angler or angling writer the Northwest has produced first cut his teeth on the North Fork's summer steelhead run.

The North Fork was where Zane Grey and Roderick Haig-Brown first fished for steelhead, and it was in Deer Creek, the North Fork's principal tributary, where each succeeded in landing his first steelhead.

The North Fork was the river of Enos Bradner, Walt Johnson, Ken McLeod, Wes Drain, Lew Bell, Frank Headrick, and many other famous fishermen. Thanks mainly to the efforts of Bradner and other early members of the Washington Fly Fishing Club, the North Fork became the first steelhead river anywhere to be placed under fly-fishing-only management, a status it has enjoyed since 1941.

What made the North Fork especially unique was the great run of summer steelhead that ascended it to spawn in Deer Creek, and although that run has been all but destroyed by logging abuses, a hatchery program has kept the river populated with at least some summer fish. Now it is not uncommon to drive along the North Fork on a summer afternoon and see license plates from half a dozen states or Canadian provinces at the fishermen's access areas. If the Northwest has a single river that qualifies as an angling shrine, the North Fork of the Stillaguamish is it.

But there have been many changes to the North Fork since I first wrote of it. Its valley remains unrivaled for its pastoral beauty, but there are more homes and fewer farms along the river now. Summer weekends bring swarms of people to float the river in rubber rafts, inner tubes, kayaks, and canoes, and of course there are more fishermen every day of the week, so that it is much harder now to find a place to fish in solitude. The Boldt decision on Indian fishing rights has revived the spirits of the little Stillaguamish Tribe and its members now fish the river with their nets, and although they fish mainly for salmon, many steelhead inevitably fall victim to their monofilament mesh. Logging continues in the Deer Creek watershed, with its disastrous impacts becoming ever more evident, and together all these things have increased pressure on the river and its precious fishery.

Simultaneously some threats have eased. A plan by the Army Corps of Engineers to build a dam at the little community of Oso appears finally to have died a quiet death, as it should have long ago, and the big timber on upper Boulder Creek—another main tributary of the North Fork—now is safely preserved inside a wilderness area established by Congress. Efforts to gain a small measure of additional protection for the river under the National Wild and Scenic Rivers Act have been stymied by lack of support from the local congressman, but such ideas have a long life and congressmen do not remain in office forever, so there is still hope.

But the biggest change has been in the people of the river. The anglers who first cared and fought for it and secured its reputation have grown old and their ranks are thinning. Lew Bell and Al Knudson both are gone, and although Ralph Wahl and Frank Headrick still visit the river from time to time, they rarely fish it any more. The row of cabins along the river below Deer Creek, once owned exclusively by these and other Stilly "regulars," has changed hands or been handed down to members of a younger generation, most of whom do not have the same deep feeling for the river or its fish.

It is this transition from old hands to new which has most affected me, for I have been a part of it.

At first the North Fork was just one river on a list of many that I fished, and although I had proper respect for its colorful history, it held no more affection for me than any of the others. True, it was the river where I had nearly landed my first steelhead, but that long battle finally had been won by the fish, and along with the fish I had lost any chance for the special sentiment a victory would have given me. To me the North Fork was merely a pleasant place to fish and a handy place to go, near enough so I could reach it after work and fish several hours on a long summer evening.

But that was before my first visit to Bucktail Camp.

Bucktail Camp was the name of one of the cabins in the row below Deer Creek, probably the smallest cabin in the lot. It was owned by Enos Bradner and Sanford (Sandy) Bacon.

It was Bradner who first took me there. We had spent most of the day prospecting for steelhead on the upper river, but late in the afternoon we drove downstream and turned off the main road onto a pair of muddy ruts that led a short distance through the woods to a little cabin perched on the edge of a small clearing. It was a plain and simple cabin, hardly more than a hut, 15 feet square and raised up on blocks in a hopeless effort to keep the winter floods from entering. It had a peaked roof, the shingles overgrown with moss, and a rusty stovepipe that belied the fact there was no stove inside. Over the single door was a large sign with the words "Bucktail Camp" inscribed in the wood. Stuck in its side was its namesake—a faded bucktail fly.

Bradner was an old man even then and fished the river less often than before, and Sandy Bacon had moved away to Oregon to retire. As a consequence the place had suffered from neglect: There were cobwebs in the windows, paint was peeling from the outside walls and a large family of mice had taken up residence inside. Cottonwoods, cedars, maples, hemlocks, and some huge old firs grew around the clearing, and these had sent seedlings that were rapidly reclaiming it for the woods. The woods made the place seem distant from everything, though it was barely half a mile from the old general store at Oso. There was no telephone and no water, except what could be dipped from the river, but a fisherman's wants are simple—and this place had everything a fisherman could want.

The clearing was in a hollow, separated from the river by a dike that was overgrown with swordfern and salal, huckleberry and wild rose, osoberry and Oregon grape. On the other side of the dike the river had built a large sand bar, and it had been there long enough for horsetail, thistle, and cottonwood seedlings to take root in it and begin to grow.

Beyond the sand bar was some of the best water the North Fork had to offer. Just downstream was a place called the Elbow, once one of the most famous pools on the river; here the river made a nearly right-angle turn, tumbling down over a series of gravel terraces, then merging into a fine tongue of current split by Volkswagen-sized boulders. For many years it had been Bradner's favorite pool, and although the river had since filled in some of its best holding water, it still yielded an occasional fish. Below it was the Upper Rip-Rap Pool, also sometimes called the Stump Pool, one of the longest reaches of good fly water on the North Fork, deep and fast and with room enough to hold at least a dozen steelhead at a time. Upstream was another good stretch called the Pocket, where a long run of broken water dissolved into a gleaming slick that was made to order for a riffle-hitched dry fly. And above that it was only a short hike to the famous pool where Deer Creek plunges into the North Fork.

These were the places we explored in the dying light of that long afternoon, and I listened closely as Bradner recited tales of memorable contests between men and fish in these waters. We caught no fish ourselves, but I came away with a deeper understanding and appreciation for the river and its history. And I envied Brad for owning such a place as Bucktail Camp.

So a few years later, when Brad offered to sell Bucktail Camp to me, I was absolutely delighted. He was in his 84th year then, and though he still fished often from a boat, the river had become too much for him to wade. He had written Sandy Bacon, who had agreed the place would be of little further use to them, and they had decided it was time for someone else to use and care for it. I was their choice if I wanted it.

I took my family to see the place and they fell in love with it at once and on Labor Day weekend 1976, we met Bradner at Bucktail Camp for a picnic and to hammer out the details of the transaction. We quickly agreed on the terms and shook hands on the deal, and once our business was concluded Bradner settled back to tell us something about the history of the place.

At some point in its history the land had been used as a gravel quarry, which explained its conformation. After that it had been a dump, which explained the faded bits of old glass and rusting metal that turned up in every shovelful of earth. Then it had been part of a family farm, which was subdivided by its owners shortly after World War II. Nearly all the subdivided lots eventually were acquired by the fly fishermen who by then already had made the North Fork a famous place.

Bradner had been away at the time the Bucktail Camp property was offered for sale, covering the atomic-bomb tests at Bikini Atoll for *The Seattle Times*, so Bacon handled the purchase. When Bradner returned from the Pacific, the two built a wooden floor in the clearing to serve as a platform for a tent. A trap door in the platform concealed a barrel hidden underneath which was used as a cache for equipment and supplies. A hole was dug in the moist earth of the nearby dike to serve as a cooler, and that was the extent of the original camp. Some years later the existing cabin had been built atop the original floor and since then many visiting fishermen had contributed to its upkeep and improvement.

When he had finished his discourse on the history of the cabin, Bradner turned to his pet theory about steelhead fishing in the North Fork, one I had heard him express often. He claimed that if, as you drove past the dairy farms along the North Fork, the cows were standing up and swinging their tails, then you had better hurry to the river for the fishing was bound to be good. But if the cows were lying down there was no need to hurry, for lazy cows meant the steelhead would be lazy, too. He espoused this theory with great conviction and claimed to have proven its validity through many years of observation, though on this occasion, as before, it was not quite possible to tell whether he was really being serious.

When he had finished defending his theory and the last cold fried chicken was consumed, we went our separate ways. But later that week we met again to sign the papers and Bucktail Camp was ours.

There was much to do around the place. We cut away the brush that had grown up around the margins of the clearing, discovering in the process an old stone fireplace that had been completely concealed by ferns and moss. The cabin got a badly needed coat of paint, though there was a startling moment when a sleeping bat fell out as we moved the "Bucktail Camp" sign to paint behind it. The rusty old stovepipe gave way to a new and larger one, and this one was connected to a new fireplace in the cabin. Rock and sand were hauled up from the riverbank to patch holes in the road, and an old wooden bench at the base of a big fir overlooking the river was braced to hold the weight of resting anglers. Trails were cleared and leaning trees were cut and a modest treehouse was built for the children.

With trepidation, we plugged in the old refrigerator in the cabin—Bradner had bought it used for ten dollars years before and its motor had been submerged in the waters of several winter floods—but it started up and soon chilled the beer.

But it wasn't all work. Our labors were interspersed with long walks along the river, where we often saw deer and nearly always saw at least one heron fishing motionlessly in the shallows. We found bits of soapstone and river jade among the gravel, and in the spring there were sweet wild strawberries to be picked and eaten and a winter's supply of new driftwood to be gathered for summer campfires. Sometimes when we paused in our work we could hear grouse drumming in the woods or an osprey calling as it searched the river for its prey, and we soon found that Bucktail Camp was a community all itself, with shrews and squirrels and lizards and robins' nests and hollow trees where woodpeckers made their homes. And every weekend, when we left the cabin, the mice would move back in.

And then there was the fishing.

The best of it was gone by the time we became the owners of Bucktail Camp, but there were still moments when it was good, sometimes even great, and only rarely did I wade the river without faith that I would find at least one fish if I looked long and hard enough—even on days when the cows were lying down. Two kinds of steelhead returned to the river, the slender, gleaming, streamlined fish of the native Deer Creek run, and the stockier, heavier fish from the state rearing ponds upstream. A fish of either kind was always welcome.

But I got off to a slow start in my first full season on the river. In fact, I was in a terrible fishing slump, having gone for months without hooking a single steelhead. I was still looking for my first fish from the waters around Bucktail Camp when I came upon Walt Johnson fishing the foot of the Rip-Rap Pool near darkness on a July evening.

Walt is among the last of the old corps of Stillaguamish veterans who still fish the river faithfully and in recent years he has become something of a legend, both for his prowess with a fly rod and for the stealth with which he comes and goes. Like the deer along the river, he is most often seen at twilight or at dawn, moving softly through the woods to emerge and take up a stance in one of his favorite pools. When I found him he was casting a long line and a dry fly, and I settled down to watch—a rare chance to glimpse a master at his craft.

He soon noticed me there and we began to chat while he continued fishing. Then a big steelhead rolled far down in the corner of the pool, and

Walt's fly was over him like a shot, floating down over the spot before the current had swept away the ripples from the rise. The fly passed over unscathed and Walt plucked it smartly from the water and cast again, but the result was the same. Several more times he cast, and although the fish rolled a second time, it was not in pursuit of the fly.

Walt reeled in. "What kind of line do you have on?" he asked.

"A sink-tip," I said. I had been fishing earlier, but as usual without success.

"Well, you'd better get out here then. This fish isn't going to take a dry, but I'll bet you could take him on that line."

"Oh no," I said. "That's your fish."

But Walt already was wading toward the beach. "Wade out there, just above that break in the current, and cast down to him," he said.

I followed instructions and waded to the spot, then stripped line from the reel and tried to gauge the distance to the last place where the fish had risen. Then I began to cast.

Now our roles were reversed and Walt was watching from the beach. "You're going to get yourself a fish, Steve," he said in such a way that I believed it.

But after half a dozen casts my confidence began to wane. The fish had not shown itself again, and I resolved that if something didn't happen after the tenth cast I'd leave the pool and let Walt try again.

The steelhead took on the ninth cast. The fly came to a sudden hard stop as if it had found a snag where none had been before, and I reared back and felt the weight of a heavy fish. It jumped only once but put up a long and sullen fight and I handled it carefully in consideration of the light leader I was using, but finally beached it in the quiet water below the Rip-Rap Pool. It was a bright silver buck of about ten pounds.

The darkness was nearly total by then, but Walt was still watching and I carried the fish up to him and thanked him as best I could for his generosity in yielding the pool and giving me the chance to catch it. We stood and talked until the darkness was full and a soft rain had begun to fall. As we parted, I thanked him again and told him that I'd been in a terrible slump and this was my first fish in a long while.

"This fish will break the slump," he said. "You'll see." Then he vanished into the woods while I began the walk back to Bucktail Camp, the fish hanging heavily from my hand.

Next morning the rain was still falling and fat clouds filled the valley clear down to the firtops. I stayed in the cabin during the morning to tie flies, but when the overcast showed no sign of lifting I finally put on a rain jacket over my fishing vest and hiked up to Deer Creek. No one was fishing at the creekmouth, so I waded out carefully over the big, slippery boulders in order to cast down to the point where the current from the creek merged with the North Fork's main flow.

After just three casts I was into a steelhead that raced downstream out of the pool and into the long Deer Creek Riffle down below. I waded ashore and stumbled over the toaster-sized boulders that littered the beach in an effort to follow. Looking downstream, I saw an older fisherman I knew was hard of hearing and for an instant I was afraid he wouldn't hear me coming, but at the last moment he turned and saw me. His eyes widened and he reeled in quickly and backed out of the way.

The steelhead finally ran itself out and I beached it midway down the riffle. It was a Deer Creek fish, slim and bright and probably no more than five pounds, but it was full of spite and spunk as Deer Creek steelhead usually are.

I released the fish and went back up to the head of the riffle to resume fishing. The current at the head was swift and it was hard to hold a fly in it for any length of time, but there was one place where the current curled around a boulder, leaving a quiet patch of water just below. I dropped my fly in that little pocket and a steelhead seized it instantly.

The fish ran downstream and once again I found myself on the beach, stumbling over rain-slickened boulders in breathless pursuit. Then the fish began to jump, giving me a chance to catch up with it, but after its third leap it fell back squarely on the leader tippet and broke it.

So I lost that fish, but I didn't really mind. Counting the fish from the night before, I had hooked three steelhead in five casts—something I'd never done before and have never equalled since. And after that day, I've always considered Walt Johnson a pretty fair prophet in addition to his other talents.

There have been many other exciting moments during the years since that first summer at Bucktail Camp. The 1980 season was the best of all; that year the river swarmed with steelhead all through the summer, and old-timers said it was the best they had seen since the war. Why it was so good is a question that confounded even the biologists responsible for managing the river, but whatever the reason it lasted only that single year; next season steelhead were few and far between.

Over the years I've grown to know the moods of the North Fork in both good times and lean. Early in the season, when the water is high and cold and fast, the river is hard and uncomfortable to fish, but often it is most generous then. The fishing is easier in August when the water is low and clear, the current slow and big rocks are showing like the bones of some prehistoric beast, but that also is when the river is most difficult and unyielding. Still, there are times in August when steelhead will rise to a riffle-hitched dry fly, and if there is a more exciting sight in fishing I have yet to see it.

The North Fork also is a different river in the morning and the evening and at midday. In morning, when the sky is just beginning to lighten in the east, the river seems new and full of promise, as if it had been reborn overnight; but later, in the heat of the day, it grows languid and lazy and the summer sun glares fiercely from the surface of its pools. Finally, in the evening, as darkness spills down the valley like a rising flood, the river becomes mysterious and alive, with trout rising in the shallows, bats plunging to feed on the twilight hatch and the slap of a heavy salmon leaping in the quiet water of a distant pool.

No matter what time of day I visit the river I rarely fish alone, for the North Fork's fishermen are many and not all fish with rod and reel. They include the herons, most patient of all fishermen; the kingfishers, perhaps the most impatient, and the ospreys, surely the most spectacular fishermen of all. I enjoy fishing in their company and do not begrudge them their success, for I admire them and I know they are entitled to their share of the river's yield as much as I am.

But unhappily both for them and for me, the fishing trend in the North Fork has been inexorably downward in recent years—with the marvelous exception of the 1980 season. It is now obvious that the steelhead run is in serious decline and that its decline is but one symptom of a multitude of problems, most related to the continuing mismanagement of the Deer Creek watershed. Each winter the creek sheds massive loads of silt into the North Fork and great drifts of it have piled up behind every rock for many miles downstream. Silt has filled the crevices of the river-bottom gravel, rendering it unsuitable for spawning, and has covered gravel bars, hardening into lunar landscapes in the summer sun. So much silt has been washed down that it has filled the riverbed to the point that the North Fork no longer can carry all the water that seeks to use it for a channel, and when Deer Creek floods—as it does now several times each winter—the river often overflows and spills out into the adjoining fields and farms.

This has happened at least three times in the past few years, a little worse each time. All three floods have filled the hollow of Bucktail Camp and reached inside the cabin, but fortunately the damage has been small and miraculously the aging refrigerator still runs.

Even in summer a brief shower is enough to turn Deer Creek an ugly ruddy brown—some anglers say a hard sweat would be enough to knock Deer Creek out of shape—and a heavy rain destroys all fishing in the lower river for days on end. The silt drifts that fill the river also make for dangerous wading, and altogether the North Fork has become less hospitable both for fishermen and fish.

Anglers have watched all this happen and have known the reasons for it, but in a state long dominated politically and economically by logging interests, the casual destruction of watersheds has almost become a way of life; little was said about Deer Creek and nothing was done. Of all the state or federal agencies that might have intervened, only the state Game Department—a poor stepchild of state government—showed any interest, and that interest was confined mostly to periodically cataloguing the decline of the native steelhead run. That decline finally reached such alarming proportions that in 1983 the department imposed a 30-inch minimum size limit on steelhead caught in the North Fork below Deer Creek in hopes of assuring the return of a few more of the smaller Deer Creek fish. It was largely a token gesture, however, since many North Fork "regulars" already had long been in the habit of releasing most or all the fish they caught.

But then a young Forest Service biologist named Jim Doyle began to take an interest in the problems of Deer Creek. He made a survey of the condition of the watershed and a public meeting was called to hear his report.

The meeting was held on a spring evening in the Fire Station at Oso. Early arrivals found seats on folding chairs, but as more and more people came they began lining up against the walls; some even stood outside in the rain and listened through an open door. Walt Johnson was there, and Ken McLeod, and many of the river's other less famous personalities. Of the three major landowners in the watershed, the Forest Service and state Department of Natural Resources both were represented, but the Georgia-Pacific Co., the major private landowner, did not bother to send a representative. Biologists from the Game Department and the Stillaguamish and Tulalip Indian Tribes were there and so were many local landowners and fishermen. Rain drummed steadily on the roof and a few hundred feet away Deer Creek was high and roaring.

Doyle began by showing color slides he had taken in the watershed, numbing images of landslides, washouts, ravaged slopes and gutted streams, a realm of destruction that in some cases resembled that left by the eruption of Mount St. Helens.

Doyle explained that Deer Creek and its tributaries originally had cut their channels through unstable glacial silt and clay. So much of the watershed consisted of this unstable soil that natural landslides undoubtedly had occurred long before man first set foot in the area, and these slides probably had kept the silt load in Deer Creek at a near-critical level even in its natural state. Still, the amount of silt entering the stream under natural circumstances had not been so great that the stream was unable to carry it away, and the pristine Deer Creek managed to remain healthy and clear.

When logging began, most of it was in the lower watershed where slopes were not so steep and the impacts not so great. But as those areas were turned into graveyards of rotting stumps and slash, the loggers were forced to begin cutting timber on higher ground. They built more roads, which added to natural erosion, and began logging steep hillsides, which accelerated it even more. The faster runoff and erosion began filling Deer Creek and its tributaries with more silt than they could handle.

The streams probably would have suffered even if proper forest-management practices had been followed, but they suffered much more because they were not. Doyle's survey turned up a sad litany of abuses. Among them:

— Insufficient buffer strips had been left along streams. Instead of providing cover and protection, as they were meant to do, trees in the strips had blown down into the streams, gouging out soil from the soft banks and adding to the erosion problem.

— Logging roads were built without proper drainage, or with culverts that were too small, resulting in washouts. Even when culverts of proper size were installed, they had been damaged and left unrepaired, or had become plugged up and were never cleaned. Result: More washouts.

— So much forest cover had been removed that during warm weather the water temperature in portions of Deer Creek was reaching levels dangerous to trout.

— Logging slash had been left in natural runoff channels, causing more washouts and erosion.

— Slash burns had been allowed to get out of control and become so hot they literally "cooked" the soil in portions of the watershed so that nothing could grow in it.

— Protective measures written into timber-sale contracts or specified by state guidelines had been neither observed nor enforced.

The cumulative effect of all these abuses was greatly increased and more rapid runoff and erosion, leading to sporadic flooding of Deer Creek and increasing the width-to-depth ratio of the stream. In other words, the farther Deer Creek flowed, the wider and shallower it became, until at low water it was very nearly dry, devoid of pools or enough water for fish to live in. Steelhead spawning and rearing habitat on the creek and most of its tributaries was rated at zero.

The most pressing problem was a huge slide emanating from an area that had been logged off years before. The slide, fed by springs, was pumping a kind of silt slurry into Deer Creek which promised to keep the lower North Fork unfishable all year long, perhaps for years to come.

The Forest Service, meanwhile, was planning to build another 16 miles of logging roads and clear-cut another 1,000 acres of the upper watershed.

As a result of his findings, Doyle proposed a monitoring program to try to document the decline of water quality and fish runs in Deer Creek. Then, if the results so indicated, perhaps the agencies responsible for managing the watershed could be persuaded to leave what was left of it alone. It was a rather feeble proposal, but with senior Forest Service bureaucrats listening in the room it took no small amount of courage to make it.

The audience listened with a mixture of sadness, frustration, and fury, and the meeting finally broke up with no clear sense of accomplishment or purpose. But it caused enough of a stir to get others interested in the plight of Deer Creek: *The Seattle Post-Intelligencer* and *The Seattle Times* both published extensive articles. The state Game Commission approved an emergency resolution extending the 30-inch minimum size limit downstream from the confluence of the North and South Forks all the way to salt water. And the state Department of Natural Resources, while hastening to disclaim all responsibility for the latest slide, sent in work crews and heavy equipment to divert it at least temporarily and assure one more summer of fishing on the North Fork.

But the future remains as murky as the waters of Deer Creek after rain. There is yet no long-term commitment on the part of any agency to improve current management in the watershed, let alone to stop cutting timber or begin a restoration program; on the contrary, there seems to be much more interest in escaping blame or liability for everything that has happened. The official bureaucratic line is that there is no proof logging has had anything to do with the flooding, erosion, or siltation of Deer Creek or the disappearance of the steelhead—although logging is the only activity that ever has taken place in the watershed and it's hard to see how any reasonable person could possibly conclude that the damage was caused by something else.

It is especially sad when one considers that the value of the timber removed from the Deer Creek watershed almost certainly has been worth far less than the value of the fishery destroyed in the process. At best, timber can be harvested only once every 50 to 60 years; the fishery, if left to itself, would have produced a handsome annual yield to the local economy, easily surpassing the one-time value of the timber harvest in the long run. To be sure, Deer Creek is not an isolated example of such false economy, but the destruction of its unique summer steelhead run makes it an especially outrageous one.

It would be less than fair to say that Deer Creek is responsible for all the North Fork's ills. Poaching also is a serious and growing threat, and on any given weekday the number of legitimate fishermen on the river probably is a minority compared to those using weighted hooks, spears, guns, or other illegal methods. Most, but not all, are local fishermen, and most of them know better, but the authorities seem unwilling or unable to do anything to stop them. The situation is now out of control.

As this is written, the state Game Department is preparing for yet another count of the number of adult summer steelhead returning to Deer Creek. This time, however, the purpose of the count is to determine if the run is on the verge of extinction. When the results are in, a decision will be made whether it is worthwhile to trap the few remaining fish and spawn them artificially in hopes of keeping the genetic stock alive until Deer Creek may again be fit for spawning or rearing summer steelhead. The alternative may be that the run will have to be written off as a resource too far gone for saving. It is not a pleasant choice, made less so by the fact that either alternative would give the timber companies and their subservient management agencies free rein to do as they please in what remains of the watershed.

Even if the native fish somehow should manage to survive, either on their own or with help, it will take many years to heal the damage that already has been done. Even then it is unrealistic to expect that Deer Creek or the North Fork ever again will be anything like the cold, clear, steelhead-filled rivers that Zane Grey, Roderick Haig-Brown or Enos Bradner fished. Those of us born too late to enjoy those happy times must take our satisfaction from what remains.

Bradner himself made his last visit to Bucktail Camp in his 90th year. There was no fishing that day—the occasion was a picnic with family and friends—and there are photographs commemorating the event. They show a group of happy faces, with nowhere a hint of realization that the day might signal the end of an era on the Stillaguamish.

After the photos were taken and the table was cleared, Bradner climbed the dike one last time and stood under a big fir and looked at the river for a long time. His legs were stiff and unsteady, his frame was bent and frail, but there was still the look of eagles in his eyes as he gazed at the Elbow Hole and remembered what it had been like when both he and the river were young.

In January 1984, Bradner passed away quietly in a nursing home where he had spent most of the last year of his life.

That spring, on a dark rainy afternoon in May, there was another gathering at Bucktail Camp. A few members of Bradner's family and two old friends met at the cabin, greeted one another, then walked together down the path to the edge of the Elbow Hole. And there they scattered the old fisherman's ashes over the water he had fished so long and loved so well.

When they had finished, they returned once more to Bucktail Camp and stood before the fire to drink a final toast to their relative and friend.

And now he belongs to the river.

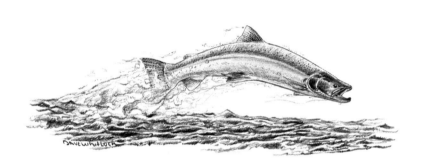

Blackberry Run

I discovered Blackberry Run early on an August morning when the air was fresh and cool. At the time I didn't know its name, but I could see at once that it was a classic stretch of steelhead water, made to order for the fly.

At its upper end the current hustled down through a narrow chute, then fanned out in a long even flow against the base of a high rock bank covered with berry vines—the namesake of the pool, as I would later learn. Breaks and swirls on the surface gave hints of big boulders and hidden pockets down below; surely this was a place where summer steelhead would stop to rest and seek shelter on their journey home.

Downstream a thick layer of morning mist floated in the valley, but overhead the sky was blue and brightening with the onrushing light of day. I chose a fly from the collection in my box, then waded out and took position in the flow.

At first I searched the water close at hand, watching carefully as the large dry fly bounced along on the current, hoping a fish would rise to meet it. But I had fished only a little while before the sun's disk topped the serrated ridges to the east and lit up the layer of mist a mile downstream. Then the light advanced upstream as the sun rose higher, and I began hurrying my casts to cover as much water as I could before sunlight stained the pool.

I made a long cast across current and dropped the fly near the high bank on the far side. The fly floated only for a foot or two before a steelhead came in a sudden rising wave and took it down. I set the hook and the fish jumped immediately, out of the shadow and into the advancing sunshine.

It was not a large fish but it was strong and active and quickly took the old Hardy St. John twice into the backing. Four more times it jumped, then made half a dozen lesser runs before I led it slowly to the beach. It was a fine native fish, a buck of five pounds or a little better, and the big hair-wing fly was stuck firmly in the corner of its jaw.

I worked the fly free and slipped the fish gently back into the river and waited until it was gone. Then I fished down the remainder of the run, raising nothing more, and by the time I had finished the sun had warmed the air and the day had turned lazy. But it was a fine start for an unfamiliar pool, and I knew I would return.

Naturally it was with great expectations that I did so, but the circumstances were far different from before. It was still August, but this time it was near the end of a misty day, already growing dark as I found the path leading down to the river. The path led through a gallery of ancient firs, standing as tall and straight as the masts of a sailing ship, with a few old cottonwoods scattered among them, bent by years of wind. Together they groaned and creaked in the evening breeze and dripped the day's accumulated rain, so that my fishing vest was soaked by the time I left them.

The rain also had fueled the river so that it was much higher and faster than before. It seemed dark and unfriendly in the fading light, and I guessed that a dry fly held no prospect in its current mood. So I chose a sinking line instead, and knotted on a small dark fly.

I waded in near the foot of the chute, stripped line and rolled out a short initial cast, then added length with each succeeding throw. I had fished down just a little way below the chute when something grabbed the fly and pulled the line rudely from my grasp. Then the fish was in the air—once, twice, three times—and back in the current, running hard. At first it took my breath away, and then it took my line. I held the rod high and headed for the beach.

But it was a long way back to shore and I struggled to keep my balance while the river teased me with slippery gravel and a strong, uneven flow. Meanwhile the fish was gaining line and when I finally made it to the beach I could not tell where it had gone.

I reeled in and the backing came easily, followed by a long length of line. But then the line came tight against unyielding weight and I thought surely I'd lost the fish around a snag. I waded out, sliding my fingers down the line, following it under the surface until I felt where it was caught firmly on a rock. With arm immersed, I groped until I found the leader butt. Suddenly there was a great throbbing movement at the other end, the leader came free and the fish, still hooked, surged out into the center of the run.

This time it chose to run upstream and for the first time I thought I had a chance to gain control. It jumped again, and through the misty rain I caught a silver glimpse of it. It was a very large fish, perhaps the largest steelhead I had ever hooked, and the sight of it destroyed the confidence I'd briefly felt.

It turned then and headed downstream at a furious rate, so that again I had to follow. Then came another jump and once more I was awestruck by the fish's size. After that we traded line, back and forth, for what seemed a very long time, but gradually the fish began to tire and yield. Carefully I led it from the main current into quiet water and began to look around for a place where it might be safely beached.

But then it ran again, as strongly as before, and the run ended with a high and tumbling leap. I had expected this and dipped the rod to give it slack, but the fly still came away. When I got it back I saw the reason why: The hook had been forced open so that the point was at right angles to the shank.

I felt the icy pang of disappointment as keenly as a knife, and for a long time I stood there, with the river curling round my knees, and stared at the wrinkled gray surface of the Blackberry Run. Perhaps I thought I could somehow will the river to deliver up my fish, but it merely mocked me with the whisper of its flow. Finally I waded out of the pool and started back along the path through the dark woods, where the limbs still dripped their saved-up rain.

Now the seasons have gone their way and August and its fellow months are buried under autumn leaves and snow. But I tell myself it won't really be so very long before August comes again.

And when it does, I plan to go back to Blackberry Run.

Summer

Fall

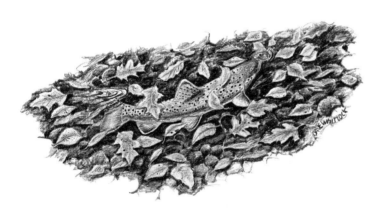

T he cottonwood leaves are the first to fall. They turn pale yellow in the August sunshine and spiral down in the easy breezes of the afternoons. The alder leaves soon follow, joining those of the cottonwoods to form a dry carpet that crackles underfoot on the paths leading down to the rivers. In the rivers themselves the trout grow restless as they recognize the signs of the changing season.

Each morning is a little cooler and each night a little longer than the last, and constellations not seen for many months begin rising once more in the east. And then one morning there is a touch of frost on the meadows, a certain sign that autumn has arrived. The farmers take in their last harvests from the fields and cut the cornstalks down to stubble; the deer that foraged so boldly in summer blend suddenly into the autumn foliage and are seldom seen again; the geese fly south in ragged formations against a pale blue autumn sky.

At first fall rests upon the land as lightly as the morning frost, but then its grip tightens. The settled weather of late summer gives way to a succession of uncertain days, with sun following rain and sudden gusts dislodging the last tenacious leaves. Every creature feels the quickening pace and makes its preparations for the coming winter, and when those preparations are complete it will be time for most to rest.

But there is no rest for the trout. Fall is spawning time for the brown trout, char and Atlantic salmon; time for the cutthroat to enter the streams and wait with the summer steelhead for their own winter spawning, time for high-country rainbows to feed avidly in anticipation of their own breeding rites in the cold runoff of the spring. And far at sea the winter steelhead have heard the ancient call of instinct to turn toward home.

All this makes autumn a golden time of year for trout fishermen, and though the time is short the opportunities are many. The hazy afternoons of late October offer a last chance for fat rainbow feeding in the lakes, for cutthroat cruising in the estuaries, for a late summer steelhead still bright from the sea. But the days pass swiftly, and soon the last October caddis has lifted off the water and the last fisherman has waded from the stream.

Fall is the final movement in the great symphony of seasons, the grand climax to the fullness of the year, fading quickly to a last long dying note. And in the hush that follows, winter comes.

Lahontans

Fall had come to the mountains and the leaves formed a vivid patchwork quilt of color as we headed down the Cascades' eastern slopes from Stevens Pass. Deer hunters were camped in clearings along the highway, the meadows still were wet with dew in the mountain shadows, and everywhere there was color—fiery orange vine maples, butter-yellow aspens and bright golden big-leaf maples, their leaves all consumed in the glory of dying.

We entered Tumwater Canyon, the great conduit through which the Wenatchee River makes its way down from the mountains, sliding through a stairstep series of emerald pools and silver riffles on its journey to meet the mighty Columbia. Then we drove past the fruit orchards of the lower valley with their endless regiments of trees lined up in even ranks, and the air was sweet with the heavy scent of ripening apples.

We crossed the Columbia itself and began the long climb up onto the interior plateau, the heartland of the state, with its rolling fields of wheat that look like frozen waves in a golden sea. At the sleepy little farming town of Mansfield we left the wheat behind and started out across the rocky, broken sagebrush country bordering Moses Coulee, a great channel carved by an ancient flood. Randy was with me and we were bound for a lake nestled in the north end of the coulee—a lake containing Lahontan cutthroat trout.

The Lahontan cutthroat is a newcomer to Northwest waters, but it is one of the oldest of western trout and once may have reached a larger size than any other trout that spends its life in fresh water. Its story is one of triumph and tragedy, a saga of nature at its best and man at his shortsighted worst.

That story begins at least 70,000 years ago, perhaps much earlier, when an ancestral stock of cutthroat somehow found its way south into the waters of the Great Basin in the country now called Utah and Nevada. The Great Basin is largely desert now, but at that time the climate was cool and wet and two great lakes, Bonneville and Lahontan, filled the basin. The cutthroat became residents of these lakes and their numerous tributaries.

Lake Lahontan, southernmost of the two, was larger than modern-day Lake Erie and the invading cutthroat found it well stocked with a natural population of minnows and suckers. The cutthroat soon learned to prey on these fish and once the predatory habit was established it continued for many thousands of years. It was a pattern that favored natural selection of larger and longer-lived cutthroat, an evolutionary trend which continued for millenia, and eventually the Lahontan cutthroat emerged as a super race of predatory trout, perhaps without parallel in the long history of the trout family.

But then, about 10,000 years ago, the climate of the Great Basin began its change to the one we know today. Without the usual rainfall and rivers to feed it, Lake Lahontan began to evaporate and shrink, its water level falling lower each year. Within a thousand years it had all but vanished and most of its trout had been forced to seek refuge in mountain streams and lakes, including some we know today—the Carson River and Independence, Summit and Tahoe lakes. Of Lake Lahontan itself, only two sump lakes remained—Pyramid and Walker lakes.

But of these two, only Pyramid Lake was able to maintain continuity and retain its original variety of Lahontan fishes until modern times—which meant that only in Pyramid Lake was the Lahontan cutthroat able to continue on the evolutionary course that had made it what it was. Elsewhere, the fugitive trout from Lake Lahontan were forced to adapt to the more limited diets available in the mountain streams and lakes where they found themselves, and in such surroundings their predatory habits were not necessarily an advantage. Though even today they still bear a close physical resemblance to the Pyramid Lake fish and are classified as members of the same subspecies, their evolutionary path over the last 10,000 years has been quite different from the trout of Pyramid Lake. The fish in Pyramid Lake were unique, the last survivors of an ancient race of super trout.

The cutthroat were well known to the Indians who lived first on the shores of Lake Lahontan and later on Pyramid Lake, and their modern descendants, the Paiutes, became skilled fishermen. The first white men to see Pyramid Lake, John C. Fremont and his famous scout, Kit Carson, were greeted by friendly Paiutes who brought them fresh trout which they had caught in the lake. "Their flavor was excellent—superior, in fact, to that of any fish I have ever known," Fremont wrote. "They were of extraordinary size, about as large as the Columbia River salmon, generally from two to four feet in length."

Fremont and Carson and their party camped near the mouth of the Truckee River, Pyramid Lake's largest tributary and the only one in which the cutthroat trout could spawn. But during the 1860s, less than 20 years after Fremont's discovery of the lake, logging began in the Truckee watershed, causing serious erosion and siltation. Numerous sawmills also began dumping sawdust into the river, and in 1869 a Reno newspaper reported that "millions" of spawning trout had been killed by sawdust pollution. The pollution was so bad that sometimes sawdust drifts blocked the mouth of the river and kept trout from entering. By 1875 dams also had blocked the river near Reno, cutting off as much as three-quarters of the original spawning habitat of the Lahontan trout.

But dams and pollution weren't the only problems. Completion of a railroad line made it possible to ship fresh fish to market and an intensive commercial fishery began in Pyramid Lake, involving such techniques as netting, snagging, spearing, clubbing and explosives. In 1899, a paper mill began dumping toxic wastes into the Truckee River, killing all the fish for a considerable distance downstream. Even when trout were able to overcome all these obstacles and spawn, there was no assurance their offspring would survive; each year, millions of trout fry disappeared into the growing numbers of unscreened irrigation ditches that took water from the river.

Despite all these threats, the trout still somehow managed to survive. As late as the 1880s, long after most of the upstream spawning and nursery areas were blocked or polluted, commercial rail shipments of Pyramid Lake trout ranged from 200,000 to 250,000 pounds a year, and the total annual catch was estimated at about 500,000 pounds.

The Lahontan cutthroat, including the Pyramid Lake fish, did not even have a scientific name until 1878. In that year, the second edition of David Starr Jordan's *Manual of the Vertebrates* identified the Lahontan as *Salmo clarki henshawi* in honor of H.W. Henshaw, a naturalist who had sent Jordan a specimen of the trout from Lake Tahoe. By this time the large size of the Pyramid Lake fish also had caught the eye of fish culturists, and trout removed from the Truckee River were being raised in hatcheries by the California Acclimatization Society.

The maximum size attained by the Pyramid Lake trout will never be known, but the official world-record cutthroat trout was caught in the lake by John Skimmerhorn, a Paiute Indian, in 1925. It weighed 41 pounds. Big as that was, there are reports of even larger fish having been taken in the Indian commercial fishery; Fred Crosby, a tribal fishery agent, claimed to have seen one in 1916 that weighed 62 pounds. If true, this would mean the Pyramid Lake cutthroat reached sizes even larger than the 56-pound Kamloops trout reported from Jewel Lake, British Columbia, in 1932 (but also never completely verified).

In 1938, the year of the last spawning run of native cutthroat in the Truckee River, a U.S. Fish and Wildlife Service biologist checked 195 trout taken in the Indian fishery and reported their *average* weight was 20 pounds. The 1938 run was an unusual one, however; it was the first successful spawning run in 11 years, which meant that most of the fish in it were at least that old themselves. An 11-year-old trout is bound to be large, and it is difficult to say what the average weight of the Pyramid Lake cutthroat may have been under normal circumstances. But there is no doubt that the Pyramid Lake cutthroat was capable of reaching very large size, and nothing quite like them has been seen before or since.

The fate of the Pyramid Lake cutthroat was sealed on June 7, 1905, when the gates were closed on Derby Dam, the first project of a new federal agency called the Reclamation Service, now the Bureau of Reclamation. The dam diverted the Truckee River for irrigation, and though it was built with a fish ladder, the ladder never worked as intended. It's hard to see how it ever could have worked properly, considering there often was not enough water below the dam for fish to swim upstream. A sand delta also had formed at the mouth of the river, making it difficult for fish to enter except during periods of high water.

Still, in the first few years of the project's existence there usually was enough surplus water to allow at least some cutthroat trout to spawn, and occasionally a few fish even were able to ascend the fish ladder. But then the Bureau of Reclamation increased the amount of water being diverted from the river and also began using water to generate electricity. After that spawning became more and more infrequent.

The last major spawning run was in 1927. The water that year was very high, and some trout were able to get above Derby Dam and go all the way to Reno. By then it had been so long since people in Reno had seen Pyramid Lake trout they had forgotten what they were, and when the mayor proclaimed a day of celebration in their honor he mistakenly called it "Rainbow Day."

Survivors from the offspring of the 1927 spawning formed the run of 20-pounders that returned to the Truckee River in the very last spawning run 11 years later. There might have been another, but the Bureau of Reclamation shut off the flow of the river while the trout were spawning and left them and their precious eggs to die in shrinking, stagnant pools below the dam. It was the end for the largest cutthroat the world has ever known, and two years later, in 1940, the Pyramid Lake strain of Lahontan cutthroat trout was officially declared extinct.

At the time no one fully understood just what had been lost; after all, there were still Lahontan cutthroat in other lakes and rivers. No one realized that for 10,000 years these other fish had followed a different evolutionary path; they were no longer quite the same as the long-lived, large-growing predatory trout of Pyramid Lake.

In 1950, the state of Nevada began experimental plants of trout in Pyramid Lake in an effort to replace the fishery that had been destroyed by the Bureau of Reclamation. At first they tried rainbow trout, but it was soon discovered that Lahontan cutthroat from Summit Lake and from Heenan Lake, California (where native stock from the Carson River had been introduced), displayed much better survival and growth—probably because they, like the original Pyramid Lake fish, had developed a tolerance for highly alkaline water such as that in Pyramid Lake.

But although these fish did well and succeeded in re-establishing a popular sport fishery in Pyramid Lake, they never have reached the monumental size of the lake's original inhabitants. The introduced trout have a maximum life span of seven years, compared to at least 11 for the original stock, and although they have managed to attain an average weight of eight pounds, that is still far short of the 20-pound figure recorded for the native fish in the 1938 spawning run—the only reliable record available. From this came the slow realization that the original strain of Pyramid Lake trout was so finely tuned to its environment that no other fish, not even another variety of Lahontan cutthroat, could replace it.

But there was one more strange chapter to be written in the story of the vanished trout of Pyramid Lake. In 1976, a Brigham Young University graduate student named Terry Hickman began work on a study of the Bonneville cutthroat, a rare subspecies thought to be the surviving remnant of the original cutthroat population of Lake Bonneville, which also had disappeared when the climate changed in the Great Basin. While trying to track down isolated populations of the Bonneville trout, Hickman was told that a Utah state biologist had found what appeared to be a pure strain of cutthroat in a small, unnamed creek on Pilot Peak, a 10,700-foot mountain on the western edge of the Bonneville Salt Flats. The stream wasn't even on the map, but in June 1977 Hickman set out to find it.

Packing electroshocking equipment on his back, he hiked to the reported location of the stream and found it was actually the headwaters of a creek that had been diverted to provide a municipal water supply for the town of Wendover, Utah. Above the diversion point the stream was barely two miles long, half of it in Utah and the other half in Nevada. Hickman later named it Donner Creek because it once had drained into Donner Springs, the first source of fresh water found by the famous Donner Party after it crossed the Bonneville Salt Flats in 1846.

Using his electroshocking gear, Hickman sampled the stream above the diversion and captured several fish. They were clearly some kind of cutthroat, but they were much different in appearance and conformation from the Bonneville cutthroat he was seeking.

Dr. Robert J. Behnke of Colorado State University, the foremost authority on cutthroat trout, was Hickman's thesis advisor and it was to Behnke's published works on cutthroat that Hickman turned in an effort to identify the strange fish. Of all the cutthroat subspecies described in Behnke's writings, he could find only one which appeared to match the spot pattern and physiological features of the trout from Donner Creek—*Salmo clarki henshawi*, the Lahontan cutthroat. But it seemed impossible that Lahontan cutthroat could be living in a stream on Pilot Peak, far from the ancient site of Lake Lahontan, unless they had been put there by man.

Behnke confirmed the identification of the fish as Lahontan cutthroat and a search was begun to try to find out where they had come from. No record of stocking could be found, but Behnke and Hickman were able to establish that the fish had been in the stream for a long time. A Utah conservation officer reported he had been told in 1957 by an elderly rancher that the creek "always had native trout," and the retired master of the Wendover water works confirmed that cutthroat were in the stream when he went to work there in 1952. That was before the state of Nevada began its hatchery program using Lahontan cutthroat from Heenan Lake, so the Pilot Peak cutthroat could not have come from that source.

The Nevada and Utah Fish and Game departments reported that no Lahontan cutthroat had been stocked in either state between 1930 and 1949, so the fish in Donner Creek must have been put there even earlier than that. Further confirmation came from a retired game warden who told Hickman that during the late 1940s he had stocked rainbow trout in many local streams, but never had put them in the creek on Pilot Peak because it already held trout.

So Behnke and Hickman looked back even further. Finally they discovered that in 1910 a shipment of more than a million Lahontan cutthroat eggs had been sent to several counties in eastern Nevada, near the Utah border. Other shipments apparently followed from time to time, possibly as late as 1930. It seemed probable that Donner Creek had been stocked with fry hatched from one of these shipments; there did not seem to be any other likely explanation.

But it was the source of the eggs that created the most excitement: All of them had come from Pyramid Lake. Here, suddenly and unexpectedly, was strong evidence that the fish in the little two-mile-long creek on Pilot Peak were members of the unique Pyramid Lake cutthroat strain believed extinct since 1940.

The dramatic announcement by Hickman and Behnke of their findings created quite a stir within the biological community, and the rediscovery of the Pyramid Lake fish also soon became the subject of a widely read article in *Sports Illustrated* magazine. As a result of the publicity, the Fish & Wildlife Service made plans to collect fertilized eggs from Donner Creek and transfer them to a hatchery where it was hoped they could be developed into a breeding stock. There was even talk of reintroducing the stock to Pyramid Lake, or planting it in reservoirs full of scrap fish where presumably it would revert to its old ways and grow to old age and large size.

But unfortunately that's not the way things turned out. In a recent letter to the author, Behnke explained what happened:

"The fate of the Donner Creek cutthroat trout is an excellent example of a basic problem of fishery management with state and federal agencies—lethargy and apathy in regard to trying something new and innovative," he said. "The small population in Donner Creek has been expanded and made more secure by a transplant in a neighboring stream, but no action has been taken to utilize this resource for fisheries management. Some fertilized eggs were taken to the Hotchkiss, Colorado, federal fish hatchery in 1980, after the publicity in the *Sports Illustrated* article. As would be predicted with a wild stock handled at a facility geared to raise domesticated trout, all fish died at hatching.

"As the publicity died down, and there was no outside agitation to do anything more, nothing more was done."

And so the original Pyramid Lake strain of Lahontan cutthroat trout, once thought lost forever only to be miraculously rediscovered, now has been largely forgotten again in its remote transplanted home on Pilot Peak. One can only hope that someday men will find a way to atone for their treatment of this unique fish, largest and most unusual of all western trouts, and restore it to a habitat resembling the one that made it what it was.

But while there is yet no happy ending to the tragic story of the Pyramid Lake cutthroat, other strains of Lahontan cutthroat have fared better. Their tolerance for high levels of alkalinity has made them a valuable fish in western states where there are many alkaline lakes, and Lahontan trout have been planted in many of these waters. Most of these fish have come from the Carson River-Heenan Lake strain, including the majority of Lahontan cutthroat planted in Northwest lakes.

One of these was Lake Lenore, a shallow, 1,700-acre lake located in spectacular surroundings at the lower end of Grand Coulee in Washington State. For years the Washington Department of Game had been keeping an eye on Lake Lenore, a rich water fed by underground seepage and a small creek that flowed in from Alkali Lake. Lenore always had been too alkaline to support fish of any kind, but over the years its alkalinity had slowly decreased and in 1977 the department decided to try again to see if it could find a fish that could live in Lake Lenore.

Mindful of the Lahontan cutthroat's tolerance for alkalinity, the department obtained 30 Lahontans, put them in live boxes along with a control group of rainbow trout and placed the boxes in Lake Lenore. Within 48 hours all the rainbow trout had died, but all the Lahontans were still alive. They remained alive, and though still confined to the live boxes, after a while some of them even began to grow and put on weight. Finally the 30 fish were set free in the lake and the department began searching for a reliable source of more Lahontan cutthroat trout.

Nevada was the obvious source, but its hatchery stocks had been afflicted by an outbreak of disease. No other source could be found, so for the next couple of years Lake Lenore remained barren except for the original 30 trout used in the survival experiment.

Then, in May 1979, Bill Zook, a Game Department biologist, found a pair of 19-inch cutthroat—survivors of the original 30—trying to spawn in the little stream that flows into the northern end of Lake Lenore. Struck by the possibility that a self-sustaining cutthroat population might be established in Lake Lenore, Zook commissioned a renewed search for a source of eggs. This time Nevada was able to provide 100,000 Lahontan cutthroat eggs certified free of disease. These were delivered to a pair of Washington state hatcheries where they were incubated, hatched and reared into fry. Mortality at one hatchery was very high, but 35,000 fry survived at the other and in October 1979 these were planted in Lake Lenore.

Utilizing the rich and virtually untouched food stocks in the lake, these fish—which averaged two inches in length when they were planted—grew to an average length of 10 inches by the following June. That summer the department obtained another 200,000 eggs from Nevada which produced another 135,000 fry, and these were stocked in October 1980. The lake was opened to fishing on a year-round basis with a one-fish limit, except during the spring spawning season when only catch-and-release fishing was allowed. Only artifical flies or lures with single barbless hooks were allowed.

During the winter of 1980-81, another one of the original 30 fish was caught by an angler. It measured 25 inches and weighed 6½ pounds. By that time the fry planted in 1979 had grown to an average length of 18 inches.

As Zook and other biologists had hoped, the Lahontan cutthroat soon developed spawning runs to the inlet stream at Lake Lenore. The stream is far too small to permit natural reproduction on anything but the smallest scale, so the Game Department began trapping the returning fish and spawning them artificially—a process which has now become an annual ritual. By managing the run in this way, the department has obtained enough eggs to restock Lake Lenore annually with enough left over to begin stocking other lakes.

One of the first other lakes to be stocked was Grimes Lake in the northern end of Moses Coulee, and it was there Randy and I were headed. Grimes is another highly alkaline water that never had been able to support fish until Lahontans were introduced. It is managed under the same regulations as Lake Lenore, except that it is open to fishing only from July 1 to September 30 each year because of its importance as a waterfowl-management area. That was why we had chosen to go there late in September, when the water would be cooling down just before the season's end.

We parked the truck in a dusty clearing near the lake and made a quick inspection of its shoreline, where we found hordes of little scuds hiding under rocks and noted the empty shucks of hatched-out midges floating in the surface film. Farther out we could see spent *Callibaetis* mayfly spinners resting on the surface and adult damselflies buzzing lazily overhead. Obviously Grimes Lake was rich in food for trout.

Having confirmed that to our satisfaction, we muscled the little cartop pram down to the water's edge, loaded it with our rods and other tackle and rowed up a long, narrow channel leading to the main lake. There was little sign of surface activity, but we had not really expected any; in keeping with its long predatory heritage, the Lahontan is not known as a free-rising fish. So we began fishing with a sinking line and a scud pattern.

The lake was a brilliant dark blue in the early afternoon sunlight and appeared incongruous in the dry country that surrounded it. Bitterbrush and sage grew around the shoreline and the coulee walls rose up sharply in a series of basalt terraces baked by the sun. In such warm, dry country I had expected to find the lake filled with a bloom of algae or at least a heavy growth of weed, but there was little of either; the water was surprisingly clear. I put in my thermometer and it registered an even 60 degrees at the surface—surprisingly cool for a lake in such notoriously hot country, especially at the end of a long summer.

We found a shallow bay and eased the anchor down, then started reaching out with long casts and a slow retrieve. When nothing moved to the little scud pattern, I changed it for a larger Carey Special, the staple fly of Northwest lakes. But it too went untouched, though we moved around a bit to try it in untested waters.

Then I noticed backswimmers were beginning to dart to the surface as they came up to replenish the little bubbles of air they carry with them under water, so I clipped off the Carey, put on a backswimmer imitation and began to fish it with a quick, darting retrieve to match the motion of the naturals. But the trout ignored it too.

It seemed obvious that some drastic change of tactics was in order, and I began searching through my fly boxes, hoping for an inspiration. Suddenly my eye fell upon the silver tinsel body and peacock sword wing of an Alexander, an old English pattern I had last fished many years before in British Columbia. If it caught my eye, I thought, perhaps it would catch a cutthroat's eye as well. So I removed the backswimmer imitation and replaced it with an Alexander.

The very first cast rewarded us with the sight of a large bronze shape that followed the fly as I retrieved it to the boat, but the fish turned away at the last moment. The next dozen casts brought three or four more follows, but in each case the fish finally turned away, so I tried varying the speed of the retrieve to see if that would induce a fish to strike.

At last one did; it took the fly hard and fought stubbornly in a series of short, strong rushes, never showing itself until it was thoroughly tired and I was able to lead it to the boat. It was a stout fish, all burnished bronze in color except for crimson splashes on its gill plates and a pair of prominent red-orange cutthroat slashes beneath its lower jaw. Large black spots were spaced evenly over its body, and altogether it was quite unlike any other trout I'd ever seen. It was about 18 inches long and weighed around three pounds.

A little later Randy landed another trout, nearly a twin of the first but not quite as heavy. Five or six others were hooked briefly and lost, and many more followed our flies without taking; it was obvious we had yet to find a fly that was exactly right, one they would take without hesitation. We tried other patterns, but none proved any better than the Alexander, and I regretted not having brought along a box of sea-run cutthroat flies; it would have been interesting to see if these landlocked fish would take patterns tied for their sea-run cousins.

By then it was growing dark, so we loaded up the boat and drove to nearby Jameson Lake to make our camp and spend the night. Next day we returned to Grimes Lake and fished again in hot still weather. The fishing was similar, and although again we missed many fish, we succeeded in landing trout from 2½ to three pounds, which fought in the same stubborn way. A couple of them also later proved to be excellent fish on the table.

I was glad for the chance to meet the Lahontan. It is not as spectacular as the free-spirited rainbow trout that inhabits most Northwest lakes, but its potential for reaching large size and its long and interesting history make it a welcome addition to the local angling menu. Not only that, but it has provided fishing in waters where formerly there was none.

I, for one, plan to take advantage of those new opportunities.

Notes from New Zealand

When a trout fisherman visits the South Island of New Zealand he is obliged to try his luck on the Mataura River. The Mataura is probably the South Island's most famous stream, an amazingly productive river that can be wonderfully generous in yielding fat brown trout to a skillfully fished dry fly or nymph. But when I arrived on the South Island early in the Southern Hemisphere autumn, the Mataura was high and dirty from a long summer of heavy rain. One glimpse and I knew it would be unfishable for days to come.

In search of an alternative, I asked around in the friendly little town of Gore, which straddles the Mataura where it makes a nearly right-angle turn and flows from east to south. A helpful clerk in the local sport shop referred me to the Pomahaka River. It was a stream I'd never heard of, but he assured me it was fine dry-fly water with a fall run of seagoing brown trout that came up from the much larger Clutha River, of which the Pomahaka was a tributary. It sounded tempting, so I thanked the clerk, bought some flies he recommended, and set out early the next morning to find the Pomahaka.

It wasn't an easy river to find, but after exploring several back roads around the village of Kelso in the hills north of Gore we came at last to a small sign that said "Anglers' Access." Beyond it was a dirt track leading across a sheep paddock to a row of willows. We followed the track beyond the willows and found the river, next to a grassy clearing that was such a perfect natural campsite that we decided to spend the night even before I sampled the fishing.

Once camp was set up I assembled a rod and explored downstream for half a mile or more. The Pomahaka turned out to be an utterly delightful stream, small, moderately clear, easily wadable and almost every inch of it fishable. But in that half-mile of water I didn't see a single rise, and though I fished with dry flies, wet flies and an upstream nymph, I hadn't had a single strike by the time I returned to camp for lunch, wondering if the river really did hold trout.

During lunch I noticed the stiff breeze which had been blowing all morning was beginning to subside. I glanced upstream and saw a trout rise in a stretch of slow, deep water. That rise was quickly followed by a second, then a third, and within moments the river was dotted with rising fish. I finished my sandwich in a hurry, picked up my rod and began wading upstream to a point where I could reach the nearest rises with a cast.

Then the breeze picked up again, riffling the surface of the stream, and the rise stopped as quickly as if someone had thrown a switch. I put my dry fly over water where moments earlier a dozen trout had risen, but not a single fish would come up to greet it.

That was my first lesson in the finicky habits of the Pomahaka's trout.

Later that afternoon I hiked upstream and found the water got better and better the farther up I went. It was classic dry-fly water, with deep riffled runs cutting under clay banks and willow roots along the river's edge, forming all kinds of sheltered holts for trout. I fished two pools bordered by spectacular sandstone cliffs, both showing marks of fresh erosion by the wind. Even while I fished, a sudden gust of wind dislodged a volley of rocks from the top of one cliff and sent them showering into the pool, frightening any trout that might have been lurking there.

Where there were no cliffs the river was bordered by rolling paddocks full of docile sheep or willows full of brightly colored birds. In one willow-bordered pool I found a fat, beautifully marked brown trout of at least three pounds that had found a good feeding station off the tip of a protruding willow root. I did all the right things, or at least all the things I thought were right, creeping cautiously through the brush to a spot well below the fish, then casting carefully upstream so that my little fly would float down over him. At first the trout was tolerant of this, but its patience finally waned and it moved off slowly into deeper water without once rising to the fly. And if ever a trout conveyed contempt by its posture or movement, this one did.

A little while later I found another, rising periodically in the center of a riffle, and this one took my fly and I landed it easily. It wasn't large—not big enough to mount, but still large enough to count—and it was my first-ever brown from a South Island stream.

That night I looked in my dictionary of the native Maori language for the meaning of the name Pomahaka. As nearly as I could determine, "death chant" was a reasonable translation—a grim-sounding name for what seemed such a pleasant river.

Next morning there was another fine rise of trout in the big slow pool above our campsite. Small mayflies were coming off the water and tiny cinnamon-colored ants were falling into it. I waded across the river and climbed a hill on the far side, and from that vantage point I could see a winding channel through the center of the pool, a foot or two deeper than the surrounding water. About a dozen trout were cruising up and down the channel, rising occasionally either to the mayflys or the ants, or perhaps to both. They were big fish; the smallest was at least two pounds, the average maybe three or four, and there was one brute that looked as if it might weigh as much as ten pounds—almost certainly a sea-run fish.

I left the hill and made a careful approach to within casting range, and for the next two hours tried nearly every fly I had. Once or twice a fish tilted up to take a look, but none even came close to taking. By then I had decided they were feeding selectively on ants, but I had not brought any ant patterns with me from the States and had seen none among the flies in the tackle shop at Gore. (Later, after examining fly selections in many other shops, I concluded there probably was not a single size 18 cinnamon ant in all of New Zealand.)

Later that day, after the frustrating rise had ended, I met some of the people who live and fish along the Pomahaka. First was a remarkable fisherwoman named Irene Kennedy, who paused in her pursuit of trout long enough to share a cup of tea and tell us about a nine-pounder she had taken from the river a week before. Though that was our only meeting, Irene became a faithful correspondent and we still keep in touch years later. Such are the friendships made along rivers.

Next was Bill White, another local angler. He had taken a five-pounder that very morning, but only after showing it 21 different fly patterns—something I could easily believe. When he opened the fish he had found its stomach stuffed with the tiny ants I had seen upon the water. The fish finally had taken a Greenwell's Glory—White didn't have any ant patterns either.

Then we had a visit from Bill Thomson, owner of "Camperdown," the farm on which we were camped. We asked his permission to spend another night on the river. "It's God's river," he said, "and you have as much right to be here as I have." Like our other visitors, he was warm, generous, and friendly, and we soon learned that is the natural way of the rural New Zealander.

Later I resumed fishing and came upon a freshly fallen tree lying across the river. The foliage was still attached and three large trout were lined up below it, sipping tiny insects that seemed to be falling from the leaves. I couldn't tell what they were, and had nothing that small anyway, so for lack of something better I put on a size 16 pale yellow mayfly pattern which resembled some naturals I had seen hatching earlier. I dropped the fly close to the fallen trunk and immediately a trout came up and sucked it in. But when I lifted the rod there was no answering pull—somehow the trout had escaped being hooked. The disturbance of its rise put down the others, and as it turned out that was as close as I would come to taking one of the Pomahaka's larger browns.

But I did not feel as if my fishing had been without reward. The Pomahaka is a beautiful and charming river, even though its fish are difficult, and I remember it fondly and think of it often. And one day I hope to return.

* * *

When we left the Pomahaka and drove down from the hills we found the Mataura still dirty with runoff from a thousand farms and fields. So we followed the highway that parallels the Mataura west of Gore and turned off at one of its tributaries, the little Otamita, in hopes of finding fishing there. The road followed the stream and the stream led it into a narrow little valley where there was scarcely room enough for both. At the far end of the valley the sky was dark and fat with the promise of more rain.

The Otamita looked clear, but it seemed a limpid little stream without much spirit or vitality. Its banks also were lined with brush so thick that we could see the water only now and then, and it seemed there was no place that offered casting room. But then we rounded a curve and came to a point where the valley widened and the river formed a broad, magnificent pool. Its far side was bounded by a nearly vertical slope, but next to the road it was just a short drop down a grassy bank to the edge of the stream.

I parked our rented van on the roadside and got out to survey the pool, just in time to glimpse a slowly spreading circle of water where a trout had risen. Small mayflies were riding down on the slow current and as I watched I could see trout rising in at least half a dozen locations in the pool.

But there was something else in the pool: Sheep were grazing on the impossibly steep hillside across the stream, and three of them apparently had lost their footing and tumbled down to the river; now their woolly corpses were half submerged in the pool. One trout, which appeared larger than any of the others, had taken up station next to one of the sheep. Even as I watched the trout tipped up and took a fly, leaving a heavy bulge of water that lapped against the flank of its dead companion.

The flyfisher encounters countless problems on the stream. The pages of angling literature offer good advice on how to deal with most of these, and if you read enough you will find the correct answer to almost any conceivable set of circumstances. But I had never read or heard of a proper way to float a dry fly past the far side of a dead sheep in the middle of a pool. This was definitely a problem that called for some sort of innovative tactic.

I studied the situation and decided the best approach—indeed, the only one—would be from upstream. A careful slack-line cast just might succeed in a drag-free float past the half-submerged sheep. But there would be only a single chance, and the odds seemed long against success.

With rod in hand, I worked my way slowly and cautiously down through the deep grass until I dared go no closer to the stream. The trout rose again next to the dead sheep and I mentally calculated the distance, then rose to a half crouch and began working out line in a quick series of false casts. Finally I let the fly go, without much confidence in the result.

But the cast fell right on target, just a few feet above the fish, and the current carried the fly slowly downstream in a perfect natural float. I could see it getting closer and closer to the sheep, and just when it seemed inevitable that the fly would catch in the water-soaked wool, the trout rolled up and took it cleanly. I lifted the rod, felt an instant's weight, then nothing. The fish was gone.

When I inspected the fly I found the hook was broken at the bend. It was then I realized that my backcast must have ticked the fly against a concrete utility pole behind me on the roadside. New Zealand has few trees suitable for making poles, so concrete is often used instead.

Dead sheep and concrete utility poles—two unexpected hazards of angling in New Zealand. Slowly I was learning that fishing in this far-off land was not quite the same as it is at home.

*   *   *

A fisherman in New Zealand, or anyone who spends very much time outdoors in that lovely country, can hardly fail to notice the wonderful variety of birds. Birds colonized New Zealand long before men and for eons had the place nearly to themselves (New Zealand's only native mammal is a bat). In the absence of any land-based predators, some birds evolved into flightless varieties, such as the giant moa, now extinct, and the shy, nocturnal kiwi, which has survived to become the national emblem. Others evolved in myriad different ways and brought a wealth of beauty, sound and movement to the skies and forests of their adopted land. Since the arrival of European settlers, many foreign species have been introduced, but none is quite so colorful or interesting as the native forms, and it is impossible to go anywhere in New Zealand without being in range of a host of chiming, chattering, musical birds.

Some New Zealand birds, like the kiwi, are so reclusive they are seldom seen, but others are so intensely curious one can scarcely fail to notice them. The bush robin is one of these.

I met the bush robin one morning while prospecting for trout along the margins of the South Mavoran Lake. It was a gray autumn morning and the season's first snow had left a gleaming white mantle on the beech forests that cover the crests of the surrounding hills. The light was poor, but with polaroid glasses I could catch an occasional glimpse of large trout patrolling close to shore. I was staring intently after one of these when I felt a tap on the shoulder. Turning, I found myself eyeball-to-eyeball with a female bush robin.

As New Zealand birds go, the bush robin is far from the most attractive. It has a head that looks too large for its body and a body that seems too large for the long, spindly legs that hold it up, and the female's feathers are mostly a dull, nondescript shade of brown. But its very homeliness, plus its uninhibited friendliness and curiosity, make it a strangely appealing little bird.

This particular robin had settled on my shoulder as if it had been invited there. We stared at one another for a few moments until I decided I rather liked having it there. And it stayed with me as I went on fishing, its solemn little eyes watching intently everything I did. Finally it flew away but stayed close by and followed when I started back for camp, and when I found a piece of candy it came quickly to take it from my hand.

Later, while fishing the upper Eglinton River, I made acquaintance with another bush robin. This one came from the woods and perched on my fly rod, remaining there until I began to cast. It was just one attraction in a day filled with many, for the upper Eglinton is one of the most beautiful streams I have ever fished. It flows out of the stillness of Lake Gunn into a narrow channel of golden gravel that cuts through a dense forest of native bush, giant ferns and big old mountain beeches. The water is as clear as breath, and though at this point the stream is too small to hold very many trout, it is worth fishing if only just to see. The beeches along the Eglinton are home to clusters of wild parakeets, as bright and vivid as Christmas-tree ornaments, and it is a marvelous thing to see them and hear their songs.

Beyond Lake Gunn a narrow, twisting road leads through the mountains to Milford Sound, a spectacular fjord that opens to the Tasman Sea. En route the road passes through a long, one-way tunnel bored laboriously through a granite massif. Traffic halts outside at either end to await a green-light signal to proceed, and the waiting areas are favorite spots for the kea, New Zealand's mountain parrot.

The kea, named after the sound of its call, is a large and handsome bird. It appears mostly green while at rest, but in flight the undersides of its wings flash with iridescent crimson. It also is a curious bird—at least that is true of those which hang around the tunnel portals—and will take food from your hand, though it is a bit more cautious than the bush robin in doing so. But the most curious habit of the kea is its appetite for rubber; if you have nothing else to offer, it will begin chewing on your car's windshield-wiper blades or rubber window gaskets.

The lovely paradise duck is a common sight on the lakes and larger rivers of the South Island, and back in the bush you will see the cheerful fantail, which the Maoris imitate in dance. And there are many others—the tui, or parson bird, so named for its white collar; the bellbird, famous for its ringing song; the tiny little rifleman, and the pukeko, an improbable swamp hen that looks like a big blue chicken—to mention just a few. A fisherman is never far from one or more of these, and their company is just one of the many attractions of fishing in New Zealand.

*   *   *

The Clutha is one of the mightiest of South Island rivers, perhaps the mightiest of all. A full-fledged river at its birth, it flows out of Lake Wanaka, one of the great interior lakes of the South Island, and winds southeastward to the sea. In its lower reaches the Clutha and its tributaries host runs of seagoing brown trout and quinnat salmon and in its upper portions there is good fishing for large resident rainbow trout and browns. But perhaps the best fishing of all is just at the point where the Clutha first becomes a river, spilling from the lake in a rush of water several hundred yards wide to start its long fall toward the sea. I camped on the shoulder of a dry hill just above the outlet, and it was there that I found some of the most exciting fishing I experienced in New Zealand.

I reached the river late in the afternoon of a fine sunny day and found a hatch of unbelievable proportions under way. Mayflies, countless thousands of them, were hatching in the lake and drifting down on an accelerating current that carried them into the river. There were whole fleets and flotillas of them, dark blue in color, some almost black, and yet their wings somehow caught the sunshine and reflected it so that the river seemed full of shining sparks. Waiting to receive them were hundreds of trout of all sizes, rolling and porpoising in the current as they captured fly after fly.

Feeling the familiar surge of excitement that comes from such a sight, I waded out quickly within casting distance of the nearest rising fish. Among the flies I'd brought were some size 16 Blue Uprights that had served me well back home; they seemed too small to imitate the naturals that were hatching here, but they were the best I had, so I knotted one to the end of my leader and began casting. The little fly floated down on the current and quickly became lost among dozens of naturals, and I realized there was little chance a fish would find it among all the real ones on the water. But surprisingly one did: After several casts, my fly disappeared in a splashy rise and suddenly I was fast to a running fish.

I headed for shore, rod held high and reel singing as the fish sought out the strongest part of the flow and used it to advantage. It fought like a small steelhead, taking the line down into the backing and once running the leader around a large rock so that I had to wade out again, reach down

Fall

173

and pull it free. But at last the trout tired and I forced it to the beach; it was a fine rainbow, nickel-bright and in perfect condition with a small head and a thick body. It weighed about 2½ pounds and I judged it was probably one of the smaller fish I had seen rising.

I rose two other fish but missed them both before the hatch began to fail at the onset of the early autumn twilight. For a while there was a lull, but then a hatch of sedges came. Like the mayflies, most of the sedges emerged in the quiet waters of the lake and were carried down by the current to the river, and soon the infant Clutha's surface was covered with fluttering, ungainly insects. I captured one and found it was about the size of a No. 10 fly pattern, with a green body and dark wings, and this time my fly box yielded a perfect match in size and shape and color. But for some reason the trout seemed less interested in the sedges than they had been in the mayflies, and only now and then did a fish rise within casting reach.

Far out in the center of the flow, well beyond the reach of any caster, it was a different story; there I could see fish rising steadily, and most of them were very large. Their rises were violent, the sounds of them audible above the sounds of the river, and they pushed water out in awesome rings. But soon it was too dark to see anything at all, and I reeled in and began the long climb up the hillside to the level spot where we had camped.

The next day was cool and overcast and the mayfly hatch did not repeat itself. Rises came occasionally and sporadically, but I fished patiently and eventually rose a fish to a local dry-fly pattern I had bought in a tackle shop in the little town of Wanaka. At first the fish ran strongly, but then it settled down to fight in a series of short rushes, never showing itself, and from this behavior I deduced it was a brown. And so it proved to be when I beached it, a handsome male of about four pounds, all freckled and speckled and tawny-gold in color, with a prominent kype on its lower jaw.

Toward evening the sedge hatch came on again, as thickly as before, and in the brief frenzied moments before darkness I rose and hooked another good fish, but held it only briefly before the fly came away.

That night was cold and clear with a brilliant display of all the southern constellations, but the following morning was overcast and cool. Gradually the monolithic clouds broke themselves up into fragments and the fragments went their separate ways and by noon the autumn sun was shining and a gentle breeze was riffling the surface of the river. Again there were no mayflies, but every now and then a solitary sedge came drifting down from the lake and disappeared in a heavy rise far out in the center of the flow. I went exploring, and at length I found a convoluted course over which I could wade out farther than I had ever gone before. The current was strong and the water lapped dangerously close to my wader tops, but I was out far enough to reach some of the rising fish with a long throw.

The fish were wary and selective in the clear water and when nothing came to a fly fished at the end of a four-pound-test tippet I switched to one whose breaking test was only three. Things began to happen then: A trout rose twice and I covered it with a long cast; the sedge imitation floated over the fish and it rose and took the fly confidently. I tightened and felt a heavy weight, but only for a moment. Inspection showed the fish had snapped the three-pound tippet with scarcely any effort. It was not a case of knot failure; the tippet was broken cleanly, halfway up.

I put on a new tippet and another fly and resumed casting. The fly soon disappeared in a large bubble surrounded by a swirl. I set the hook and the fish started off on a long downstream run, and I began the long, difficult wade back toward shore—a move that quickly proved to be a bad mistake. I was going one way and the fish another and the backing peeled off the reel at an alarming rate. The line formed a giant belly stretching far across the river, all at the mercy of the current; finally the pressure was too much, the leader parted and the fish was gone.

I began to despair then of ever holding a fish in the heavy current on such a light leader. Nevertheless, I waded out to try again and quickly rose another fish but missed the strike. A few casts later came another rise, the most spectacular of all, from a large fish that lunged at the fly and threw up a fountain of spray. Like the others, it started immediately on a downstream run that went swiftly into the backing and brought joyous sounds from my old Hardy St. John reel.

Remembering what had happened earlier, I resolved this time that I would stay where I was instead of trying to wade ashore. And when the trout's initial run was over, I was able to lead it slowly back upstream until I had it on a short line and everything seemed under control. But then the fish began to jump, revealing itself as a big rainbow. It jumped eight times in succession, throwing itself far out of the water each time, and on the eighth jump the fly came away.

After a few more casts it was time to go, for we were due back in Christchurch to catch a plane to the North Island. My score for the day was not impressive—four fish risen, three hooked, two broken and one lost. But it had been wildly exciting fishing and I had thoroughly enjoyed every moment of it. I also took comfort from the thought that success, like beauty, is measured in the eye of the beholder, and one standard of success in fly fishing is the ability to fool large and difficult fish with a floating fly. By that measure it had been a most successful day.

*   *   *

An American fly fisherman in New Zealand has certain advantages over local anglers, particularly if he is well equipped and knows the double haul. By well equipped, I mean that he should have his own pair of chest waders, which will allow him to gain access to waters seldom fished by local fishermen. Chest waders are very expensive in New Zealand, where so many such things must be imported, and as a consequence not very many anglers have them—particularly on the South Island. They use hip boots instead, and while this does not penalize them on the smaller streams, it certainly does on big rivers like the Clutha. While fishing there I was able to wade out far beyond the local fishermen, all of whom were wearing hip boots.

The long-distance casting technique known as the double haul also is rarely seen in New Zealand, despite the fact that most anglers there use long rods and many use shooting-head fly lines designed for use with the double haul. A visiting angler who knows this casting method can easily reach water well beyond the range of the best New Zealand single-haul caster. Again this advantage holds true only on large rivers and lakes, but there are many of both in New Zealand and it is a mystery to me why the double haul never has caught on there. Among all the fishermen I met during two long visits to that country, I encountered only one who was a good double-haul caster.

Many of New Zealand's best waters are reserved for fly fishing only, a happy circumstance that stems from the angling preferences of those who settled the country and developed its early trout fisheries. There is probably some abuse of these regulations, but generally they seem to be well respected by those who fish with other methods. Perhaps other anglers realize that fly fishing is the method most consistent with preservation of the resource, which is a matter of great self-interest to New Zealanders—not just because trout fishing is an important part of their local way of life, but also because it provides a significant source of foreign exchange for their country.

The classic kind of fly fishing, with dry flies and nymphs, is mostly in the beautiful streams of the South Island. North Island fishing is mostly done with sinking lines and large wet flies, or "lures" as the Kiwis call them. The fishing is not as good as the tourist promotions would have you believe—it never is, anywhere—but it is still very good indeed. It is seldom fast but is nearly always interesting, entertaining and rewarding, and the average New Zealand trout is much larger than its counterpart in most stateside lakes and streams. It also would be difficult to conceive of surroundings more lovely than those awaiting the angler in New Zealand.

Using British traditions as their base and making imaginative use of local materials, New Zealanders have developed their own distinctive school of fly-tying theory. This is especially true on the North Island, where tyers have created many unique feathered "lures" for trout in Lake Taupo or the Rotorua lakes. Some of these, such as the Matuka and the Hamill's Killer, now are becoming popular on North American waters and others probably will follow suit. They are, for the most part, large, colorful flies combining clever blends of feathers, fur, and tinsel. Most are what we would call "attractor" flies, many designed for use at night. Relatively few of these patterns were conceived as imitations, and if New Zealand fly tyers lag in any one respect it is probably in the science of exact imitation.

That first became clear to me when I was fishing Lake Taupo during the "smelting" season, a time when schools of smelt move into the shallows and large rainbows and browns come in to feed on them. It is a wonderfully exciting kind of fishing, with the large trout usually visible in the clear water so that you can watch them follow the fly right up to the moment of the take. But though I fished a wide variety of local patterns tied to imitate the smelt, none succeeded in matching it very well, and a truly consistent or effective pattern seemed to be lacking. In part, this may be due to the difficulty and expense of obtaining synthetic materials in New Zealand; I think a local tyer with access to the same variety of synthetics that North Americans take for granted could soon fashion a smelt imitation that would be deadly.

But the lack of good imitations also extends to the dry flies used on South Island streams. Here again, exact imitations are few and most patterns are tied according to traditional formulas now considered out of date in most other parts of the world. The small selection of dry flies that I brought from home served me much better than the local patterns I was able to obtain, although that may have been due partly to the fact that I fished them with more confidence.

New Zealand now frowns upon visiting anglers who bring their own flies or fly-tying materials and will not allow them past customs without fumigation—a regulation intended to protect trout from diseases prevalent in other lands. But I do not think this ban would apply to synthetic materials still in the package, and if I return to New Zealand—as I sincerely hope to do—I will take along some of these together with some basic fly-tying tools, then rely upon the local shops to furnish whatever else I need.

For a country of small population with a trout-fishing tradition that goes back scarcely a hundred years, New Zealand has developed a remarkably rich body of angling literature. Some of it is known in North America and more of it probably ought to be.

One of the best-known New Zealand titles is O.S. "Budge" Hintz' *Trout at Taupo*. Lesser known, but just as much worth reading, is his later work, *Fisherman's Paradise*. Hintz, a retired editor of *The New Zealand Herald*, is a gifted writer with a fluid style that vividly captures the moods familiar to fishermen everywhere. His favorite stream, celebrated often in his writing, is the little Waitahanui, a tributary of Lake Taupo. If you should see it from the highway bridge on the eastern side of the lake you might easily wonder how someone could find so much to say about such a limpid little river. But if you explore upstream you will soon find out: The Waitahanui in its middle reaches is deceptively swift and deep, a captivating little stream that hurries down through hills covered with brush thickets and criss-crossed by anglers' trails. A rainbow hooked in its swift current is twice the fish that you expect, as I learned to my satisfaction. The Waitahanui may be small, but it is a river that fully deserves a great writer to sing its praises.

By North Island standards, the Tongariro is a giant river, one whose fame has spread across the globe. It too is a river that deserves a heritage in print and it has found one in Tony Jensen's *Trout of the Tongariro*. Jensen lacks the practiced literary style of Hintz, but his book is a fine, straightforward, pool-by-pool account of the Tongariro, the very model of what a fishing guidebook ought to be. Although now retired from his guiding days, Tony Jensen had a remarkable knowledge of the river, which he demonstrated one day when we fished together on the Duchess Pool. Tony pointed toward a little wrinkle down toward the tail of the pool and well on the far side, and said that if I would wade to a certain point and cast so that my fly would swing through the wrinkle at a certain angle, I would hook a trout. He didn't say I *might* hook a trout; he said positively that I would. I did as he said and hooked a trout exactly where he said it would be. An autographed copy of his book now occupies an honored spot in my library, and I have read it many times.

John Parsons' little book, *Parsons' Glory*, is another excellent New Zealand title, a collection of the author's newspaper columns filled with Kiwi fishing lore and legend. Yet another is *The Flies in My Hat* by Greg Kelly, which receives my nomination for a prize as one of the best-titled fishing books in any language.

Keith Draper's *Trout Flies in New Zealand* is the most exhaustive work in print on that subject, and Rex Forrester's *Trout Fishing in New Zealand* is the most useful all-around guide a visiting angler could wish to have. And there are many other titles that could be mentioned.

New Zealand's cities and towns have many bookstores—more than you would find in any North American city of comparable size—and it is worth a fisherman's while to spend time in as many of them as he can. There he will find some treasures worth as much as the fishing itself.

*   *   *

Nearly every river flowing into Lake Taupo has a "picket fence." That is the term New Zealanders have coined to describe the fishermen who line up shoulder-to-shoulder off the river mouths to cast into the rips where the current from the river mingles with the quiet water of the lake. Most of this fishing is done at night, and most of the rivers have their own faithful cadres of fishermen who return to them night after night. Off the mouth of the Waitahanui, scene of the most famous picket fence, there is often a lineup of wading anglers in the daytime as well.

It is not the sort of fishing that interests most visiting American anglers. Indeed, the very term "picket fence" conjures up images of the kind of fishing mob scenes that are becoming all too common on many North American trout streams, and when an angler travels 6,000 miles to fish in New Zealand a mob scene is the last thing he expects. More than once I've heard American anglers say they would never be caught standing in a picket fence, and I suppose I once felt that way myself. But that was before I tried it.

I remember thinking that the picket fence was, after all, a part of Taupo angling tradition, and I had read many warm tales about such fishing in the books of Hintz and other New Zealand writers. I decided that as long as I had the opportunity, it might be something worth trying once, just for the experience. Besides, my stay in New Zealand was drawing to an end, and joining a picket fence for an evening's fishing seemed an ideal way to extend the angling day.

I was staying at an inn not far from the mouth of the Tauranga

Taupo River, which had its own picket fence like nearly all the others. But the lake off the mouth of the Taurango Taupo is too deep to wade, so its picket-fence fishermen come in boats each evening and anchor parallel to one another in a line at the farthest reach of the river's current. The inn's proprietor had a rowboat which he offered to let me use, so I made plans to join the Tauranga Taupo picket line.

It was late in the afternoon when I set out on the short row to the river's mouth. The sun was headed down toward the blunt, broken shape of Mount Tongariro on Lake Taupo's western shore and the great lake was absolutely still, stretching away like a vast plain of glass to distant horizons. Looking over the side of the boat I could see the volcanic sand of the bottom at great depth; I had fished Taupo years before but had forgotten how marvelously clear it is.

Two boats already were anchored in position off the river's mouth as I approached. They were parallel to one another at close quarters with a single angler casting from one and a pair fishing from the other. Being somewhat uncertain about the etiquette of such fishing—especially what was considered the minimum acceptable distance between boats—I eased my craft next to one of the others and waited for somebody to say something. But the other fishermen merely nodded in greeting, so I nodded back, dropped anchor and began to fish.

From the reading I had done I knew the usual technique was to make a long cast, let the fly sink and then retrieve it slowly. It's far from the kind of fishing I most like to do, but it's the way most Taupo trout are taken, and I soon got into the long, leisurely rhythm of it.

More boats began to arrive and get in line as the afternoon wore on toward evening. But there was no scrambling for positional advantage; the newcomers merely extended the line and were welcomed cordially by the others. Most seemed to know one another and soon they were all involved in a lively conversation with much good humor. Some of their questions and comments were directed my way and I realized I was being invited to join the conversation—even though my Yankee accent clearly marked me as a stranger. But I did join in and quickly found myself thoroughly enjoying the conversation and the company, and soon I did not feel like a stranger any more.

The sun gleamed off the still water until about 5:30 p.m. when it set behind the high western hills. The twilight seemed only seconds long; one moment the sun was shining brightly and the next there was only a milky-blue glow to mark the place where it had set. A little onshore breeze came up and suddenly it was very much colder.

I had been fishing a smelt pattern without response—none of us had even had a strike—but with the sudden change in temperature and light I stopped fishing long enough to put on a heavy sweater. It also seemed a good time to change flies, so I replaced the smelt imitation with a Red Setter, one of the most famous and colorful of local patterns.

It had been dark only a few moments when one of the others announced he'd felt a fish's touch. Then another fisherman's rod bent and bucked and his reel began to talk as a trout took out line. The others offered verbal encouragement as the fight progressed, and after a few minutes a fat rainbow was writhing in the lucky angler's landing net.

Then it was my turn. Suddenly the line was snatched from my fingers and a strong fish was running with it. After the initial run we traded line back and forth a while, but the fish never showed itself and I began to wonder if it might be a brown trout. But the strength of its rushes soon convinced me otherwise.

Eventually the fish tired and the others cheered when they saw the fight was coming to an end. I had no net, but when the trout came alongside I seized it by the lower jaw and lifted it into the boat. It was a rainbow, about 22 inches long, steel-bright and almost obscenely fat—a typical Taupo trout. There were warm words of congratulation from the others.

I caught nothing after that, although one or two more fish were taken by the others. Finally it was late, and time to go.

I rowed slowly away from the others until they faded from sight in the darkness and I was alone on the still surface of the great lake. The lights of Taupo town twinkled far across the water, 30 miles away, and overhead the sky was ablaze with stars whose light was old long before it reached my eyes. The stately Southern Cross was there, and the curious luminescent patches of the Magellanic Clouds, and by their faint light I could still see the silver volcanic sand on the bottom far below. Here and there a trout ripped the surface as it fed, but there was no other sound.

Suddenly a spectacular meteor flashed overhead, leaving a glowing trail that was visible for 30 seconds after it had passed. I marveled at the sight and thought how ironic it was that an object that may have drifted aimlessly through space since all the worlds were young should suddenly encounter the atmosphere of this small, out-of-the-way planet and die in such a momentary blaze of light.

I gazed up at the heavens from which the meteor had come and at all the legions of stars still shining there, reflected also in the still water around my drifting boat, and in the silence I wondered if another fisherman could be adrift on some dark and distant lake out there—a fisherman who even now might be looking up and thinking thoughts that were similar to mine.

Such are the feelings that Taupo inspires on a still, clear autumn evening.

I returned to the Tauranga Taupo picket fence several times after that, and by watching and listening to my new friends I learned many of the subtleties and secrets of rivermouth fishing—and there are more of these than meet the eye. Later I joined a picket fence of wading anglers off the mouth of the little Waimarino River, which has its own group of regulars. They were as friendly as the others and just as generous in sharing their knowledge, and one night when they were late arriving I discovered that I greatly missed their company.

I caught more fish, though the fishing never was especially fast, and after a time it became clear to me that for the local anglers the fishing was almost a secondary thing; it merely offered an excuse for them to get together, to talk and laugh and share their friendship—even with a stranger from across the sea. I think of them often now, casting their large feathered lures far out over the still surface of the lake, then chuckling softly to one another in the autumn dusk, and I wish I were back among them.

Someday, with a little fisherman's luck, perhaps I will be.

Fall Favorite

The sea-run cutthroat is known as a blue-collar fish, a tough, no-nonsense trout that hangs out on the waterfront, down around the docks or in the brackish lower reaches of short-run coastal streams. Those are tough neighborhoods, and maybe that's why the cutthroat seldom travels alone; it almost always has a few buddies along. Considering its wrong-side-of-the-tracks reputation, you might think the best bait for cutthroat would be a shot and a beer. But despite its plebeian image, the sea-run responds willingly to flies; in fact, it's a much better fly-rod fish than most anglers suppose. And it is one of my favorite fish in the fall.

The sea-run cutthroat bears scant resemblance to its landlocked cousins of the interior basins. After a summer of feeding in the estuaries its sides are typically as bright as a switchblade and its back is a cold blue-green. It wears a buckshot pattern of fine black spots and the cutthroat slashes that are the badges of its breed are faint like a pair of faded scars. When hooked on a fly it fights stubbornly, usually in a series of short rushes, but it sometimes jumps well and always displays surprising endurance, no matter what its size.

Those cutthroat destined to spawn in winter enter the rivers in the fall, and that is where most anglers seek them. But there are always bright fish remaining in the estuaries, fish that feed through the fall and winter and well into the following year, and a small clannish band of anglers searches for them there. These estuary anglers bring a certain amount of fanaticism to their task; they must be prepared to fish in rain from cold gray dawn to bitter dusk, to endure freezing fogs or bone-chilling winds or even squalls of snow. That's the kind of weather cutthroat like.

A Puget Sound cutthroat fisherman follows a familiar set of tactics developed over many years. He patrols the beaches, sometimes on foot but more often in a boat, and casts out among pilings or over oyster beds where cutthroat like to feed. He uses a sinking line and bright, gaudy flies, and when he sees the swirl of a feeding cutthroat he covers it quickly and strips in his fly with a rapid retrieve. Sometimes, if he is lucky, a cutthroat will take the fly; more often it will not.

Those also were the tactics I followed when I first began fishing for sea-runs. I caught fish now and then, which seemed to be about as often as anyone caught them, but before very long I realized there was a great deal more to estuary fishing than merely catching fish. I had fallen under the spell that seems to capture every sea-run angler sooner or later—a strong feeling of attraction for the great open spaces and gray-blue vistas of the estuary, for the sight of the rushing tide under a layer of morning mist, for the sound of a chattering kingfisher or the wistful cry of a lonely gull. There is something primitive and powerful about an estuary; it is a place of indistinct shapes and indefinite boundaries, a place of indefinable charms. It may be a tough neighborhood for a cutthroat, but for a fisherman an estuary is always an interesting place to be.

Still, it was the cutthroat that interested me most of all. The sea-run cutthroat is perhaps the most enigmatic of all trout; it comes and goes according to its own timetable and its own instincts, which are not for us to know. It is a neglected and little-studied fish, and what little study has been done has revealed only the barest details of its life. We know where and when it spawns and when its offspring go to sea, but we know little of what they do when they get there—except that they appear content to remain in the estuaries and feed on whatever they find there.

In time I decided to try to learn more about them—a quest motivated partly by the frequent failure of the traditional fishing tactics I had learned. It was hard enough to spend most of a day searching for a school of feeding cutthroat, but to finally find one, cover the rising fish and then have them repeatedly ignore the fly—as they very often did—made the whole effort seem an exercise in futility. So, in hopes of learning something that might improve my chances for success, I began to study the organisms that formed the bulk of the sea-run's diet and to record observations of its feeding patterns at various stages of the tide.

The first and most obvious thing to suggest itself from these studies was a change in the type of flies I had been using. After all, there seemed little reason other than popular tradition for using bright patterns like the old Skykomish Sunrise, the Dead Chicken or the Spruce. Such flies bore little resemblance to the sea-run's actual food and it seemed reasonable to think that imitations ought to work much better. The aquatic sowbug, probably the most common item in the cutthroat diet, was too small to offer much hope of successful imitation, but that still left such larger organisms as the shrimp, the candlefish, or the stickleback. I began to experiment with flies tied to imitate these things and found they worked better than the traditional patterns, but still not quite as well as I thought they should. My ratio of fish hooked to rises covered improved somewhat, but it was still not close to where I thought it ought to be. There had to be some other answer.

Thinking long and hard about the problem, I was struck suddenly by the incongruity of what I and other sea-run anglers had been doing for so long: We had always searched for signs of rising fish, which usually signaled the presence of a school, and when we finally saw a rise we unfailingly covered it with a wet fly and a sinking line. But even in salt water a rise means only one thing: that a trout is feeding on the surface, or just below. When you stop to think about it, there's very little logic in covering a rising fish with a sinking fly. Could a dry fly conceivably be the answer?

It was a radical thought. When a trout rises in fresh water it nearly always does so in order to take an insect on the surface, but in salt water there is rarely anything on the surface for a fish to take. Very few species of insects live in salt water and few of those are capable of producing anything that could be considered comparable to a freshwater hatch. True, an offshore breeze occasionally carries flying ants or mayflies out over the estuaries, but only rarely had I ever seen this happen. If natural insects were absent from the estuaries, there seemed little chance that cutthroat would rise to a floating artificial fly. Not only that, but the idea seemed contrary to everything I knew—or thought I knew—about the character of the cutthroat in salt water. It was supposed to be a rough-and-tumble, meat-and-potatoes kind of fish, one not given to the least form of subtlety. It lived in slimy places and ate slimy things and the very notion of fishing for it with fine tackle and a dry fly seemed entirely out of place.

But the fact remained that cutthroat *do* rise in saltwater, for whatever reason. Perhaps it was a manifestation of their natural curiosity, or more likely a holdover habit from their early years in fresh water. A cutthroat spends two or three years in the river of its birth before making its first migration to the sea, and in that time it must surely learn to rise and take insects from the surface of the stream; rising also is a habit that a cutthroat resumes quickly when it re-enters fresh water on its spawning run. So perhaps it wasn't completely farfetched to think that a cutthroat would not forget the rising habit during the time it was at sea. Also, I remembered all the times I had teased trout into taking dry flies on streams and lakes when there were no natural insects on the water; maybe the same thing would be possible in estuaries.

I thought about the idea a long time before I finally decided to try it. To give the experiment a reasonable chance for success, I waited for a day with optimal conditions—a good tide, reasonably calm weather and a solid overcast to make the cutthroat less cautious. In the event, the first two conditions were present but the third was lacking; there had been thick fog early in the morning, but it had given way quickly to a rare day of bright sunshine by the time I arrived at a favorite spot on Hood Canal, a giant natural saltwater arm that separates the Olympic and Kitsap peninsulas.

I wasn't optimistic; it seemed likely the sunlight would put down any self-respecting cutthroat in the vicinity. Nevertheless, I rigged up with a floating line and knotted a No. 12 dry fly to the light leader. The fly was tied with a deerhair overlay and a deerhair wing to give it maximum flotation; that was important because I wanted a fly that not only would float sitting still, but one that could be skated across the surface without sinking. Skating was a method I had used often to stimulate the interest of trout in fresh water when there were no insects on the surface.

The tide was just beginning to ebb, withdrawing smoothly and almost imperceptibly from the beach, leaving behind a layer of dark wet gravel and sagging ranks of saltwort, still dripping from the tide. The surface was flat calm and a column of woodsmoke rose lazily from a cabin on the shore, dissolving slowly in the crisp morning air. I chose a favorite spot along the beach and began casting, allowing the fly to float briefly without movement after each cast, then stripping it in rapidly so that it kicked up a little V-shaped wake as it skated over the surface.

Nothing happened for the first little while. Then suddenly a bright cutthroat leaped high out of the water near the fly. Whether its unexpected appearance had been in some response to the fly, or whether it merely had chosen that time and place to jump, I could not tell. But I took it as a sign of encouragement and cast to the spot where the fish had been.

The fly floated there untouched and I began to strip it in. Halfway through the retrieve I caught a glimpse of a brownish trout shape in hot pursuit of the moving fly; even as I saw it, the fish made a quick lunge through the surface and took the fly in its mouth. Excited, I struck too quickly and pulled the fly away. Immediately I cast again to the same spot, but the trout—if it was still there—would not come up a second time.

More confident now, I resumed casting. Soon I saw the characteristic swirl of a rising cutthroat nearby and covered it. The little deerhair pattern dropped gently inside the expanding ring of water from the rise and I twitched it once, twice, three times. There was a flash of bright silver, the fly disappeared and the rod tip dipped obediently to the pull of a fat cutthroat. After a typically stubborn fight, I landed the fish, photographed it with the dry fly still stuck in its jaw, then turned it loose.

It took a few moments for the full realization to sink in: I had taken a trout on a dry fly in saltwater, something I had never done before, perhaps even something that no one had ever done before. But whether I was the first to do so mattered less than the fact that I had done it, and now I was anxious to prove to myself that it wasn't just a fluke.

It wasn't. I caught several more fish on dry flies that day, including some that took the floating artificial dead-drift on the surface with classic head-and-tail rises like trout feeding in a limestone stream. The whole day was a revelation to me, and a display of hitherto unsuspected behavior on the part of the cutthroat.

In the years since that day I've experimented with the dry fly in estuaries from Puget Sound to the Alaska Panhandle and have found that cutthroat respond to it enthusiastically in all kinds of weather. The largest sea-run cutthroat I ever landed, a handsome four-pounder, fell to a dry fly, and the same day brought me another fish only a little smaller. Now nearly all my estuary fishing is with a dry fly, and I am thoroughly convinced that it is a much more effective method than the wet fly—even the very best wet-fly imitations I have been able to devise.

I still use the same basic deer-hair pattern that took the very first fish, although now I fish it in a larger size. But friends who have tried the dry fly in saltwater have experienced equal success on standard high-floating flies such as the Humpy, the Goofus Bug or any of the Wulff patterns. Size and color do not seem to matter so much as the ability to keep the fly afloat and moving—since the moving fly seems much more effective than a dead float.

Much to my delight, I have found that the cutthroat is not the only species willing to rise to a dry fly in saltwater. One day a heavy steelhead took my floating fly, then headed quickly for Japan. The steelhead won that bout, but the first coho salmon I hooked on a dry fly did not: It sucked in the fly with delicate grace, then fought in a succession of spectacular leaps until it had worn itself out and I was able to lead it to a net. At various times I have also hooked sea-run Dolly Varden and chinook salmon on dry flies and on a couple of rare occasions even succeeded in raising striped sea perch, which usually are dedicated bottom feeders. But the cutthroat is by far the most dependable riser, and most of these other fish came unexpectedly to my fly while I was fishing for cutthroat.

I still do not know for certain why the cutthroat rises to a dry fly in salt water, or why any other fish does so. But given the opportunity, I would rather take fish on a dry fly than in any other way, and the discovery that it is possible to do so in the estuaries has added immeasurably to my fishing pleasure. It also has proven that even a trout from a tough neighborhood can rise to a dry fly as delicately as the most sophisticated brown. And now, for that reason more than any other, the sea-run cutthroat has become one of my favorite fish of the fall.

A Fish to Remember

The steelheader's day begins in the early half-light of the dawn. The river is hidden under a rising mist that muffles the water's utterance, a gentle whisper that will grow louder with the day. The sun is only a robin's-egg glow of promise in the eastern sky behind the sawtoothed peaks of the North Cascades. The air is cool and quiet; even the birds are still. Somewhere, out in the river, beneath those rippling boils of current that glow briefly in the reflected silver light, the steelhead are waiting. They will not come to you; you must go to them.

And so you wade out into the dark river, sucking in breath at the first feel of its chill against your waders. It is still too dark to see the river bottom, but you have made the crossing many times and you follow the familiar route, planting your feet carefully, sliding them cautiously over the slick, algae-covered rocks.

Finally you are in position, at the head of a long, languid pool, and you peer through the rising mist in the hope of seeing a rolling fish, down at the foot of the pool where they always lie. None shows, but that does not mean that none are there.

The sound the reel makes as you strip off line seems extra loud, a harsh, discordant note against the gentle morning sounds of the wakening river. Casting muscles, grown stiff from a night spent in camp on a bed that was not quite long enough, quickly limber up as the long green line works farther and farther out with each sweep of the powerful rod. The fly, a dark pattern with the inelegant name of Skunk, still is fixed to the leader point where you knotted it carefully in the dusk before the last few casts of yesterday.

Ready at last. The line rolls far out across the pool and carries the fly to the deep water rippling along the high rock bank on the far side. A mend upstream, and then another. The current accepts the fly, carries it along for brief inspection and then decides to swallow it. It is gone, invisible to you now, swinging in a long slow arc through the depths. Perhaps a steelhead sees it even now, is moving to meet it, following its passage as it tumbles in the flow. But nothing happens, and when the arc has reached its end and the line is parallel to the flow, you draw it slowly back, remembering all the times you have hooked steelhead on the retrieve at the end of such a cast. But that does not happen either, so you cast again. And again and again.

So many casts. So many mornings. So many times you have returned to camp, empty-handed, with the sun well up and the day warming, your stomach as empty as your creel, ready to trade in all your hopes for a single cup of coffee. The rest of the day is made to loaf, cut wood, drink coffee, talk or tie flies, and build back the morning's faded hopes until the eagerness returns by evening. Then you go back, back down to the pool, back to the silver chute of water that feeds it, back to the bouldery stretch where the current clutches at your heels and tries to dig the gravel out from under them. Maybe the evening will bring a bright steelhead, and if it does not, then a good night's sleep will again restore the shattered hopes.

It is late in the year and the river is low. Months have passed since the sun washed the last snow from the mountain slopes, and the dry days of Indian summer have caused the flow from the headwater springs to ebb. If only it would rain, you think. Not a lot; a lot would be too much. Just enough to quicken the current a little, to inject an element of freshness to a river gone stale, to awaken the steelhead and get them moving.

But the only fall so far has been of leaves from the limbs along the river. With each afternoon breeze there are more of them, old-rose and pumpkin-colored leaves from the vine maples and smaller yellow alder leaves with spots of brown rot already on them. The river collects them, as if they were colored postage stamps in an album, and plays with them in its current, turning them so that their sides flash briefly in the light. Sometimes you think the flash is from a fish and you stare long and hard to see if it will come again. The river has had its little joke on you.

You fish through the long evening twilight and watch the surface of the shallows boil as next year's smolts dash to feed upon tiny hatching flies. An old bruised salmon rolls out in the middle of the pool with power enough to send waves lapping against its farthest edges. Downstream a heron fishes in an eddy, standing as stark and still as a bronze sculpture. Light and color ebb from the evening sky and the first stars twinkle tentatively. Now there are bats feeding on the evening hatch, and off in the woods the owls are waking. It is time to go.

Through the scrub alders that have grown up near the river's edge, along the open gravel bars, on the well-traveled trail through the spike-grass and Indian potato near the river, other anglers are returning from the day's fishing. One who has been lucky goes before you, wading cautiously out into the river's dark flow to make the crossing back to camp. One arm is held high and from it hangs the broad silver shape of a steelhead he has kept, and you feel a pang of envy at the sight. Others are waiting as the angler exits the river on the far side and they gather around him to pay compliments, admire the bright catch and ask what fly and by what manner he managed to take it. You wade across and up to them; the successful angler is grinning and pleased and you know how he feels because you have sometimes been in the center of such attention. His is the only catch among the group, perhaps the only steelhead taken on the river that day. Alas, the steelhead no longer are as numerous as they once were.

Afterward there is a late dinner and a cold beer or two and a roaring good campfire and some talk. The flame dies away slowly and the talk goes with it as those with whom you have shared the fire become transfixed by it, watching the changing light and shapes of the glowing coals. I don't know what it is about campfires, why they are as hypnotic as they are, but when it grows quiet and the fire is the only light in the darkness along the river, people stare into it as if the fire held a message of the future, like tea leaves in the bottom of a cup.

Finally weariness wins out and even the thought of that too-short bed seems welcome. As you stand up from the fire there is a quick little gust of wind that rattles the alder branches and sends a new crop of leaves spiraling to the ground. The stars have vanished; a layer of cloud has crept in. As the wind freshens, there is a hint in it of the changing season. Perhaps tomorrow will bring rain. And long after you have fallen asleep, the rain begins drumming on the cabin roof.

The next morning is dark and chill. The night's rain has subsided to a nasty drizzle, and low-lying clouds, gray and ugly, have erased the mountains. They have settled into the valley as if they intended to stay all winter, as perhaps they do, dropping their cold sweat into the river. The river itself is as dark as the clouds that fill its valley. So far the rain has brought no visible rise to the water, but the current seems a trifle quicker, the temperature a little colder. Or is it just imagination?

You cross and start in at the head of the pool, finding the stiffness lasts longer on a cold, damp morning. But it is gone soon enough, and the long casts are falling on the familiar water, the fly searching through the reaches you have often searched before.

The river is quiet under rain. No flies hatch, there are no rises in the shallows. The kingfishers have yet to come awake, the water ousels have yet to come to feed and play along the margins of the river, and it seems as if you alone are awake in a sleeping world. The gentle river charms your thoughts, and you fish down the long pool by reflex, by habit, while your mind turns to memories of other mornings, other rivers. You think how long it has been since the first fish of summer, since the June days when the rivers ran high and swift with runoff and the first bright fish headed into them; how long since the morning when your fly found a bright 10-pounder in a sheltered stretch behind a boulder and you landed it after a long, hard fight in the swollen flow. You remember the late August afternoon when the retreating sun threw long shadows on the far side of a favorite pool, and a steelhead lying in the shadow seized your swinging fly, ran to the center of the river and leaped. Forever in your mind you will see its image there, a crescent silver shape poised for a long moment high above the pool. In another moment it had found a tangled root and broken you, but the memory remains as bright as the fish itself had been.

You think again of all the rivers you have fished, of how the very names of them evoke the excited sound of water rushing over stone: Stillaguamish, Toutle, Klickitat, Wind, and many more. Each river has its own personality, its own moods, its own peculiar color, sound and strength. Some are openly friendly, always bright and clear and eager to share their secrets, their currents cool enough to make the warmest summer day seem pleasant. Others are sullen and secretive, cold and dark and strong, their broken boulders waiting like submerged, spring-loaded traps to sweep an unwary angler off his feet. Such rivers are hard to know and hard to like, and yet their rewards are often great.

And there are some rivers that never let you know exactly where you stand. On bright days they seem sparkling and friendly in the sunshine, but when a misty summer rain settles down on them they turn cold and gray and vaguely hostile. They may be generous one day and totally unyielding the next, and just when you think you have come to know them they suddenly reveal a hitherto hidden aspect of themselves. In many ways they are the most interesting rivers of all. Fishermen will tell you it is the steelhead that draws them to the rivers, but much of the appeal is the rivers themselves, each with its own challenge, problems and personality.

The bright days of summer are a pleasant time to fish, but they are but a prelude to the fishing of the fall. The earth's colors soften as the days grow shorter and the nights colder, and there is a sudden stir of movement in the forests, fields and rivers. The last of the summer fish enter from the sea and join their predecessors in the shaded pools, growing restless as they sense the nearness of their spawning ordeal. There is an urgency as the season draws swiftly to a close, and it is felt as keenly by the anglers as by the fish they seek. In the mornings and evenings and sometimes all through the day the riffles and runs are crowded by anxious anglers, their rods rising and falling as they search for one last fish before the fall rains come. In some rivers it is the time for the greased line and the sparsely dressed fly, or a riffle hitch to make the fly plow a little furrow in the surface in hopes it will lead to a sudden explosive rise or bulging surface take.

Perhaps the misty rain now falling is the beginning of the end. Perhaps it will grow heavier as the day wears on and continue for days on end. Then the rivers will quickly rise and carry the color washed from the hillsides where the trees have been cut away. A hardy few anglers still will try to pit their skill against the swollen flow in hopes the river will yield a final catch, but the odds against success are great and they increase with each day of rain. So perhaps this quiet, drizzly dawn is the last real opportunity of fall.

It comes with the sudden ferocity of a blind-side football block and an electric shock rolled into one: One instant there is only the river's weight pressing gently on the line; in the next the line has been snatched from your fingertips, the rod tip pulled viciously down to the river, and somewhere out in the long pool a steelhead is lunging violently away with your fly stuck firmly in its jaw.

It is the thing you have hoped for, the purpose for your presence at the river, the result of all your patience and preparation; but still you are never quite ready when it comes. It draws the breath out of you and almost costs you your precarious balance amid the slippery boulders of the midsection of the pool. For a moment you feel utterly helpless.

Then experience takes over. A picture of the geometry of the river flashes quickly in the mind's eye and the brain swiftly calculates the best vantage point from which to fight or follow the fish. Without thinking, you dash quickly through the fast, deep stretch which earlier you had so carefully and cautiously crossed. And as you splash into the shallows with your reel running wildly, you catch your first glimpse of the fish as it leaps high above the river in a flash of silver spray.

Stumbling over the rain-glistened rocks, you follow it, running as fast as waders will allow. Out of the pool it goes, down through a short, rocky, rushing stretch and into the smaller pool below where it jumps again, twisting in the air like a mustang trying to throw a stubborn rider.

Now the fish pauses in its flight and you gain some ground. The rod tip throbs and dips obediently to the movement of the steelhead as you scramble to catch up. Then the fish is away again, down to the end of the pool with a strong run that takes all the line you had recovered. You slip on a wet rock and thrust out a hand to break your fall; the reel spins wildly, then stops, and for a horrible moment you fear the fish is lost. But then a heavy pull signals it is not.

It goes on this way, down the length of the pool, then part way back up again, with two more jumps and several strong runs, but each one shorter than the last. Finally, with the line taut and throbbing like a bowstring, the leader is visible and below it the large silver shape of the fish. And in another moment the fish is on its side in the shallows, its gill plates flaring open and closed from its exertions, its strength totally spent. You wade out until the fish is between you and the shore, a gentle beach where the boulders have been buried under silt. And then the fish is in your hands.

It is a female, still fresh from the sea although the month is late. The black fly is in the upper corner of her mouth, the barbed hook point having punched its way through the thick membrane above the maxillary bone and found a purchase there. The fish is as bright as the river under sunlight, as clean as the moist morning air, and you know from the perfection of her that she has never known a hatchery's walls. All the dawns and dusks it took to capture her are unremembered now; your only thought is that this is a child of the river, and the river is her home.

You twist the fly free and wash the silt from her silver sides, grasp the wrist of her tail gently and turn her upright, facing into the current.

The gills still open and close, the rhythm steadier now, and you move her back and forth, feeling in her cold flesh the gradual return of strength. And then, with a sudden powerful sweep of her broad tail, she is free of your grip, swimming slowly back into the dark river from which she was so rudely taken.

You sit down on an old water-silvered log along the riverbank and realize you are as drained of strength as the fish. The drizzle falls upon your face and your hands tremble as you try to light the wet tobacco in your pipe. Tonight, around the campfire, when notes of the day's fishing are compared, you will say that you took a good steelhead and returned it to the river. And somehow there is more reward in that than in bringing home a fish.

The tobacco reluctantly takes light and the smoke rises in the rain. You sit back and sigh and look out on the river, shining darkly in the wet, gray light, looking placid now but already gathering strength from the rain falling in the hills. Another year will pass before you see it exactly so again.

Your waders squeak as you stand up stiffly from your perch upon the log. The sky remains dark, even though above the clouds and beyond the hidden peaks the sun is up. You take a last look at the undulating pool whose surface was so recently shattered by the leaps of the steelhead you have just released, a look to fix the memory in your mind. Then you start the long walk back to camp.

Was it worth it?

Yes, it was.

It always is.

The End of the Year

The year ebbs. The blush of autumn fades quickly from the hills and the first fall storms come sweeping in from the Pacific to drop their heavy freight of rain. The days give up their warmth and the darkness lasts well into morning and comes again before the afternoon is done. High on the hillsides the snowfields start to grow; next year they will become the rivers.

All the quick life of the long warm months of spring and summer has gone to rest and the hills and valleys turn dark and drab in the gray late-autumn light. The days flow past as swiftly as the current in the streams and the prospect of winter hovers like a darkening storm on the near horizon. The season is late; the old familiar cycle once more is drawing to an end.

The years rest easily on the earth, which has seen so many come and go, but they weigh heavily on men. Inevitably their toll is felt: The trails begin to seem a little longer, the current in the rivers feels a little stronger and a dry fly floating at the end of a long cast becomes a much harder thing to see. There is a reminder of all these things in the passage of a year, and perhaps that is one reason why a trout fisherman seems determined to take advantage of every last remaining day. He plans one final trip, and then perhaps one more, even though the harsh breath of early winter already is blowing through the land.

I remember one such late-season trip. It still seemed too early to think of winter, though it was cold and wet when Pat Kirkpatrick and I left the city in early-morning darkness and when we reached the Cascades summit the first light of dawn revealed fresh snow along the road. We agreed that was not unusual in the high country, but the snow persisted all through our long descent of the eastern slope. There was even snow around the Columbia Basin lake that was our destination, and we left the only tracks on the trail leading in. The air was as cold as the blade of a knife and the lake was dark and still as we launched our boats and began to fish alone.

After a while it grew even colder and crusts of ice began forming in our fly-rod guides. No trout took hold, nor did we even see a sign of one, and there was nothing to relieve the freezing monotony of the dark morning. The cold numbed our faces and fingers until finally we could tolerate it no longer; we went ashore, shook the snow from broken sagebrush limbs and built a reluctant fire. Its pale flame was a welcome sight, but though we huddled close we could feel little of its heat; the air was so bitter that even the fire seemed cold.

But we persevered, and early in the afternoon the air warmed a little and at last the trout began to stir. First there was a solitary rise far out in the center of the shallow lake; it was followed by another, then several at a time. Pat hit a fish and then I had one and before the afternoon was done each of us had caught a half dozen or more—all big, bright, hard-fighting rainbows. That night we drove to town and treated ourselves to a big steak dinner in a warm restaurant and decided the day had been well spent despite the discomfort we had been through.

Another time Ed Foss and I set out on a dark late-November day to fish for sea-run cutthroat. A cold wind drove mixed rain and snow into our faces and whipped the water to a froth so that we were forced to seek shelter along a lee shore. Late in the day, when we were thoroughly wet and chilled, we returned to the boat ramp and found a game warden in a warm car, waiting to check our licenses. His greeting was abrupt: "I've been all over this county and you two are the only damn fools I could find outdoors on a day like this." But he was surprised to learn we had both caught fish despite the weather, and by the standards of estuary fishing it had been a most successful day.

Yet there have been other days that were not so successful, days when we pushed the season or the weather or our luck a little too far, when wind or rain or snow or uncooperative trout forced a quick retreat indoors. And though such days tend to be soon forgotten, I suspect there have been more of them than any other kind.

What magic quality does the trout possess that compels men to search for it in such dark and desperate weather? What virtue does it offer to command such unwavering devotion? I can answer only for myself: I love trout because they are among the most beautiful and graceful of all creatures and because they dwell in some of the most beautiful and graceful of all places. I love them because I am a fly fisherman and trout inspired the invention of my sport; without them it would be a very different sport, if indeed it existed at all.

The trout has a way of rising to a floating fly that takes your breath away, and I love it for that and for what it will do after the fly is firmly taken. I love trout because they are honest and uncompromising creatures; no man was ever cheated by a trout. I love them because they have inspired me to seek a wider knowledge of the natural world, and such knowledge brings immense satisfaction and pleasure. And I love trout because they have led me into friendships with others who feel about them as I do, and such friendships make a man's life immeasurably richer.

A trout, by its very nature, is a thing that can only be touched and briefly held; an angler can never truly capture one or call a trout his own. If a trout is killed it becomes a lump of cold flesh, bereft of all the virtues that make it worth seeking; if it is returned to the stream, then the angler who caught it is left with only his fragile memory for a keepsake. Yet those are the only choices, and in that mysterious ephemeral quality of trout is the very magic that makes it something larger than itself: For us it becomes the fleeting fulfillment of a dream, a symbol that a man's hopes are sometimes realized—if only for a moment. That is why the trout commands such devotion from so many, why catching one sometimes is a mystical experience that strikes sparks in a fisherman's soul.

The bond between men and trout runs deep, though it is not

ordinarily a thing that fishermen acknowledge or discuss. But it is always there, and sometimes it is revealed in unexpected ways.

One such display remains vivid in my mind. I was fishing the North Fork of the Stillaguamish and had hiked upstream from my cabin to a point where I could see the Deer Creek Riffle was empty, with no other anglers in sight. The empty stream was inviting and I hurried forward, but I had taken only a few steps when two fishermen emerged from the woods near the top of the run; they were much closer to it than I was, and my heart sank when I saw them.

But there was something unusual about the pair. They were moving at a painfully slow pace, and as I got closer I could see that although both wore waders and fishing vests and carried fly rods, one was on crutches and the other was helping him swing his legs over the scattered boulders. I stood aside and watched their slow progress toward the stream; when they finally reached it, the lame man leaned on his friend and together they inched their way out until they were knee-deep in the river. Then the helper took a crutch away, leaving his companion with only one to lean on, and gently placed a fly rod in his free hand. With the remaining crutch tucked under one arm, the lame man began to cast.

It was a touching sight and my heart went out to the young man leaning on the single crutch while the river curled around him. I learned from his friend that a bulldozer had crushed his legs and this was his first outing after many months in the hospital. Chances were he might never walk again, but even such a tragic infirmity was not enough to keep him from returning to the pursuit he loved. As I watched him there, standing unsteadily in the pool, I could not help but admire his quiet courage, and I said a silent prayer that a steelhead soon would come and take his fly.

The great sorrow is that all men do not love the trout as much. For a creature that has given men so much pleasure, inspiration and reward, the trout has suffered grievously from the activities of man. Too often it has been the victim of human ignorance, shortsightedness, or greed; the evidence lies everywhere in ruined rivers, defoliated slopes, impassable dams, and polluting industries. The truth is that man has nothing so important or urgent to do that he needs to sacrifice the trout or its habitat in order ot do it—but truth is something that often is difficult for men to see while there is yet a chance to profit from the sight.

That the trout has been able to survive at the hands of man is a tribute to the toughness of its breed and to the efforts of those who have worked to preserve it. But it is late in The Year of the Trout and the future is far from assured.

November falls from the calendar like a last lonely stubborn leaf. Along the rivers the trees stand bare and bleak and dripping from the rain. In the limbs of some the eagles sit and wait, watching for the current to bring them the last of the spawned-out salmon.

The rain clatters heavily on the dead leaves that clad the forest floor and soaks down through them to the soil; soon it will re-emerge in far-off springs. Rain fills the swamps and beaver ponds in the deep woods and collects in little brooks and rivulets that mutter on the hillsides. Day after day it rains until all the springs and swamps and rivulets and brooks begin pouring their swollen discharge into the rivers. The rivers grow fat and gray and reach out to reclaim the gravel bars and empty sloughs that have been left to dry since spring. Sometimes it rains so long and hard that the rivers cannot carry the full weight of water pressing down on them; hour by hour they edge upward until suddenly they are out of their banks and running through the fields, breaking roads and threatening the transient works of men. People curse them, but the rivers are only doing what rivers have always done.

The swollen December flow brings up the first big run of winter steelhead, though their passage may be hidden by the glut of water. But late in the month, when the weather turns colder and the rivers begin to subside, there may be a chance to fish for them.

Such fishing, when and if it comes, has an unmistakable air of finality about it. There is the certain knowledge that it is the very last fishing of the year, that the steelhead—so bright and lively now—will soon be spent from spawning as their own cycle nears an end. Even the rivers seem to grow old before our eyes: We cast into the present, which exists only for the instant it takes for it to pass; then it flows downstream, forever beyond our reach, and becomes the past. Looking downstream is like looking backward from December at all the vanished moments of the year.

Some of those moments we will long remember—good times spent in pleasant places, the company of friends around the campfire, the thrill of large trout won or lost, and all the host of happy things that only a trout fisherman can know or feel or understand. These are rewards that we alone can share.

Now the winter dusk fades into darkness and the darkness brings more rain. Soon the rain becomes snow, heavy and wet and melting at its first touch upon the soil. But then it grows colder and the snow turns thick and fine and begins to stay; it collects first upon the foothill slopes, then reaches down into the valleys and finally settles slowly on the anglers' trails and empty campfire rings along the rivers.

In the softness of the snowy night the year at last steals quietly away. But time and the rivers continue flowing—and below the surface of the silent streams, the trout are always there.

Fall

201